WHY TELL THE TRUTH: AN INTRODUCTION TO THE BASIC IDEAS OF JORDAN B. PETERSON

TYLOR S. LOVINS

For Dr. Reed, who taught me that the meaning of thinking abides in the question, "What do you mean?"

AND

For Steve Lucas, whose mentorship has taught me the most important lessons of my life, and whose friendship has been an endless source of joy.

CONTENTS

ACKNOWLEDGMENTS

First, I want to thank Alastair J. Roberts, who very graciously read over numerous drafts of the manuscript, offering many helpful suggestions and useful comments. This book would not be as clear or precise without his attention. What faults remain are, of course, my responsibility.

Chris Yager designed the cover for this book, and Eric Baker suggested I write the book in the first place. Kyle Fingerhut and Steve Lucas read a few chapters of an early draft, and their comments were invaluable. Isaac Horwedel, our Thursday night discussions have been a substantial source of reflection, and they have helped me in innumerable ways. Thank you to my sister Ashley, whose support while I was writing allowed me a certain level of sustenance that I cannot put words to. This book would not exist if it had not been for their help, and I am indebted to many others, like Shane Good, Steve Heinold, Cody Rhynard, Freddy Matthes, Justin and Daniel Lain, Cody Hendershott, Chase Tibbs, Ben Garret, and Justin Clark, for the meaningful conversations and friendship throughout the years.

Lastly, I want to thank my wife, Kelli, who puts up with me and, somehow, loves me unconditionally. If I ever achieve anything in this life, it is because of you.

FOREWORD BY ALASTAIR J. ROBERTS

In his book *Serendipities*, Umberto Eco tells of Marco Polo's encounter with the unicorn.[1] Assured by the bestiaries of his day that weird and wonderful beasts were to be found in exotic lands beyond the familiar regions of the world, Polo quite expected to meet such creatures when he travelled to the East.

Polo records an encounter with unicorns in Java. However, being a candid chap, Polo shared his surprise with his readers, describing how the unicorn had confounded his expectations. Eco writes:

> [T]he truth was that the unicorns he saw were very different from those represented by a millennial tradition. They were not white but black. They had pelts like buffalo, and their hooves were as big as elephants'. Their horns, too, were not white but black, their tongues were spiky, and their heads looked like wild boars'. In fact, what Marco Polo saw was the rhinoceros.[2]

---

[1] Umberto Eco, *Serendipities: Language and Lunacy*. Translated by William Weaver (New York, NY: Columbia University Press, 1998), 55.

[2] Eco, 55.

Polo was, in Eco's words, 'a victim of his background books':[3] faced with something novel and strange, he was only able to describe it in terms of that which was familiar, in terms of the unicorn he was expecting to encounter.

Observing the many responses to Jordan Peterson, I am reminded of Polo's sighting of the unicorn. In his own way, Peterson confounds many of our contemporary categories and the expectations associated with them. He is a firm advocate of evolutionary theory, yet teaches the opening chapters of Genesis as vital truth for our times. He is one of the most prominent voices in our society against the prevailing progressive liberal hegemony, yet is an academic from one of the most liberal fields of all. He is a university professor, yet he often speaks more like a religious preacher. He is neither an orthodox Christian nor a churchgoer, yet has led numerous people to reconsider the Christian message and move in the direction of the Church.

Much as the single horn of the rhinoceros was the feature that prompted Polo to identify it with the unicorn, so there are striking features of Peterson's public persona that cause people to misidentify him. In the monochromatic world of a polarized public square, Peterson's forceful critique of the progressive left's thought, his insistent mispronunciations of their shibboleths, and his rise to prominence in the context of his opposition to Canada's Bill C-16 has led many to misrecognize him as a conservative culture warrior of the common variety. This misrecognition, coupled with the progressive left's reac-

---

[3] Eco, 55.

tive hostility to any challenging of their sacred cows, has driven much of the intense hostility with which Peterson has been treated in the media. Having challenged sacred cows, Peterson is not regarded merely as partially or even largely mistaken, but is regarded as someone who must be exorcized from the public square. Others, interpreting him in the light of his wildly popular *12 Rules for Life*, can see him as little more than a self-help charlatan.

Misrecognition is not merely common among those who are hostile to Peterson. Many of Peterson's supporters would like to treat him as a mere baiter of the left, 'owning the libs' and carrying on the culture wars. Among his Christian fans, there are those who want to present Peterson's thought as neatly aligning with and supporting traditional Christianity. Indeed, some of the impulse in certain quarters to press Peterson to affirm the doctrines of the creed seems to arise more from a need to restore our own sense of security in the tidiness of familiar categories, rather than for Peterson's sake. If only we could neatly classify Peterson, he would no longer unsettle us!

There are various points of Peterson's thought that Tylor Lovins foregrounds in this book with which I have important differences. Also, as a more conservative Protestant than Lovins, I am much more reticent in my appropriation of Peterson's approach to scriptural teaching. Nevertheless, it is precisely in receptively yet critically engaging with aspects of Peterson's thought—which I believe Lovins represents accurately in these pages—that challenge my own that I stand to benefit the most.

Discovering the rhinoceros could have expanded Polo's world in ways a misshapen unicorn could not.

Faced with such a strange creature as Peterson, people can try to force him into familiar—and safe—categories, categories that help to allay any cognitive dissonance caused by his troubling of our taxonomies. Employing Peterson's own framework, people who are overly fearful of uncertainty and chaos can hew closely to a brittle order of oppositional categories. In a culture as partisan as ours, these will often ultimately divide people into the two camps of friend or foe.

Cathy Newman's repeated refrain from her viral interview with Peterson for Channel 4, 'so you're saying that...,' was similar to the amateur medieval naturalist encountering the rhinoceros and only being able to see the unicorn. Like Polo, Newman too was a victim of her background books, which did not prepare her for encountering such an unimagined beast as a thoughtful and informed critic of egalitarianism, feminism, and other progressive orthodoxies in the wild.

If Polo were to understand the rhinoceros, he would have needed to begin with the practice of patient attention, considering the creature on its own terms before determining how to relate it to familiar categories. The same is true of those of us who wish properly to understand Jordan Peterson.

In this task, there is perhaps no better place to start than with consideration of Peterson's notion of truth, which is arguably the mainspring of his entire thought and practice. It is here that Peterson is at his most surprising, arresting, and essential, at his most animated, invested, and engaging. Once Peterson's understanding of truth has been grasped, much else about him will fall into place. It is to this crucial aspect of Peterson's thought that Lovins draws our attention in this book.

I had the good fortune to encounter Peterson's work a few years before he burst into the broader public awareness. Back in 2013, I watched a TEDx talk Peterson delivered at the University of Toronto, on the subject of potential. I had not expected much from the video, yet I was astonished to hear Peterson speak with great insight and gravitas to deep issues of existence and reality that seldom if ever surface in the public conversation. I later listened to some of his lectures on psychology, to hear his vision articulated at greater length.

Hearing Peterson lay out his thought across a range of issues in his lectures, outside of a political context or one of antagonistic debate, gave me a better sense on his own terms from the outset. When he later entered the field of public controversy, with its clamorous din of vehement dispute, I had a much better sense of what was informing his decision to speak up.

All too often in both the academy and the public square, the discussion of ideas can feel either like a vigorous yet inconsequential parlour game we are playing together, or as terrain to be wantonly ravaged by the fury of our political battles. At best, 'truth' may exist to be weaponized in the forms of 'facts'—"facts don't care about your feelings (but they might just support mine)!" However, hearing

Peterson speak with such seriousness and passion about truth and reality, he reminds us that our souls are at stake in this business of living. If only we are prepared to submit ourselves to wisdom in the study of truth and humanity, we can find direction and resilience in the terrifying storms of life. Whereas evil, suffering, meaning, truth, and goodness may seem to be relatively weightless notions to many, floating aimlessly in the zero gravity of the lecture theatre or seminar room, Peterson alerts his listeners to their moral weight, social urgency, and their importance for our souls.

Peterson's huge popular appeal can easily be chalked up to his charisma, a 'black box' or occult entity that names his draw without really explaining it. Here again, however, attention to his understanding of truth proves instructive. As Lovins demonstrates in this book, Peterson's more pragmatic understanding of truth maintains a tight connection between thought with practice. It is from the embodied manifestation of the power of this connection in Peterson's teaching that much of the forceful appeal of his position arises. People, accustomed to encountering 'truth' in anaemic and enervated forms, are startled to attention when they see someone declaring truth as something vital and powerful, as something that is profoundly integrated into and animating of the life of its bearer.

While a weak notion of truth may serve us in our partisan ideological and political squabbles, faced with the reality of suffering, it will prove insufficient to sustain us. It is not accidental that Peterson's vision has been forged in large measure upon the brutal anvil of totalitarian political forces in the twentieth century. In facing the problem of suffering, Peterson is not merely addressing the concerns of contemporary social and political discourse that tend to revolve around the maintenance of the complacency of a shallow consumerist comfort, but is unearthing dark corners of the human soul and emphasizing the need for self-mastery if we are to become people of integrity, people who can survive and overcome the worst that life and society can throw at us. Not content with encouraging persons to be well-adjusted members of a materialistic modern society, Peterson desires to equip us to withstand the sort of radical personal and social evil witnessed in communist and fascist countries over the last hundred years of history.

It should come as no surprise that a great many people who have been seeking direction and strength to endure personal suffering have found rich spiritual sustenance in the teaching of Peterson. As an alternative to the dry morsels of bread afforded by mere ideology, words of genuine truth prove life-giving and empowering.

In *The Abolition of Man*, C.S. Lewis lamented the way in which the educational institutions of his day were producing 'men without chests'. The 'chest', Lewis argued, is the 'spirited element' of man, that realm that mediates between the head and the belly. He writes:

> Without the aid of trained emotions the intellect is powerless against the animal organism…. In battle it is not syllogisms that will

keep the reluctant nerves and muscles to their post in the third hour of the bombardment. The crudest sentimentalism … about a flag or a country or a regiment will be of more use. We were told it all long ago by Plato. As the king governs by his executive, so Reason in man must rule the mere appetites by means of the 'spirited element'.[4]

Long left to slumber in a culture of acedia and the innumerable distractions of the entertainment and news media, and anaesthetized by educational institutions that neglect the souls of their charges, the chests of many of Peterson's hearers are being awakened by his teaching. People who spent much of their lives as listless ideologues and prisoners of their appetites are discovering the emboldening and enlivening capacity of truth that is addressed powerfully to the chest, re-establishing the moral concord of body and mind in a well-ordered spirit.

By exploring the beliefs, principles, and intellectual traditions that underlie Peterson's understanding and practice of truth, Lovins is doing us a considerable service. He is helping to expose the fact that Peterson's success cannot merely be attributed to his charisma and rhetorical skills, but is deeply grounded in considered thought that has been metabolized into practiced principles.

At the end of a recent interview with the British journalist Helen Lewis for GQ, Peterson was asked how he would like to be remembered. Peterson

---

[4] C.S. Lewis, *The Abolition of Man* (Québec: Samizdat University Press, 2014), 11.

paused for several seconds before declaring, 'As someone honest.' In a society enmired in palliating falsehoods, obliging lies, weaponized facts, and expedient bullshit, the courageous words of an honest man can reacquaint us all with the liberating power of truth and call us all to reengage with the rugged realness of reality.

1. THE PROBLEMS BEFORE US

"It has been almost twelve years since I first grasped the essence of the paradox that lies at the bottom of human motivation for evil: People need their group identification, because that identification protects them, literally, from the terrible forces of the unknown. It is for this reason that every individual who is not decadent will strive to protect his territory, actual and psychological. But the tendency to protect means hatred of the other, and the inevitability of war—and we are now too technologically powerful to engage in war. To allow victory to the other, however—or even continued existence, on his terms—means subjugation, dissolution of protective structures, and exposure to that which is most feared. For me, this meant 'damned if you do, damned if you don't': belief systems regulate affect, but conflict between belief systems is inevitable.

Formulation and understanding of this terrible paradox devastated me. I had always been convinced that sufficient understanding of a problem— any problem—would lead to its resolution. Here I was, however, possessed of understanding that seemed not only sufficient but complete, caught nonetheless between the devil and the deep blue sea. I could not see how there could be any alternative to either having a belief system or to not having a belief system—and could see little but the disad-

vantage of both positions. This truly shook my faith."

Jordan Peterson, *Maps of Meaning*[5]

"Our institutions are no longer fit for anything: everyone is unanimous about that. But the fault lies not in them but in us. Having lost all the instincts out of which institutions grow, we are losing the institutions themselves, because we are no longer fit for them."

Friedrich Nietzsche, *Twilight of the Idols*[6]

The consequences of Neil Postman's 1986 prophecy-turned-truth has caused more chaos than he could have imagined: "People will come to adore the technologies that undo their capacities to think."[7] Although television was the target of this particular reference—the growing ubiquity of images, the constant 2-second camera angle flashes of the television screen—what would Postman have thought of Twitter culture which, more dangerously, makes no pretense of selecting against linguistic complexity for character-limited simplicity, and has, as a result, flattened our words? As the

---

[5] Jordan B. Peterson, *Maps of Meaning: The Architecture of Belief* (London: Routledge, 1999), 460.

[6] Friedrich Nietzsche, *Twilight of the Idols and The Antichrist*, trans. R. J. Hollingdale (London: Penguin, 2003), 104.

[7] Neil Postman, *Amusing Ourselves to Death: Public Discourse in the Age of Show Business* (New York, NY: Penguin Books, 2006), xix.

online culture selects for bombast over nuance, transactions of epigrams over concepts, this may just be the logical extreme Postman envisioned over three decades ago:

> Television is our culture's principal mode of knowing about itself. Therefore—and this is the critical point—how television stages the world becomes the model for how the world is properly to be staged. It is not merely that on the television screen entertainment is the metaphor for all discourse. It is that off the screen the same metaphor prevails.[8]

Yet, we are not merely amusing ourselves to death. Creators of our major communication tools are only now beginning to understand the pernicious consequences of these powerful platforms.[9] Just as greed is a great instigator of the profit motive, the compulsion to act and be seen publicly, without mediation, propels social media engagement. Ours is not simply a time of entertainment, but of efficiency. We see this in the form of discourse now most common on Twitter: the shitstorm. Byung-Chul Han observes, "Waves of outrage mobilize and bundle attention very efficiently. Howev-

---

[8] Postman, 92.

[9] Matthew Rozsa, "Facebook's Co-founder Blasts Social Media: "It Literally Changes Your Relationship with Society"," Salon, November 09, 2017, , accessed January 05, 2018, https://www.salon.com/2017/11/09/facebooks-co-founder-blasts-social-media-it-literally-changes-your-relationship-with-society/.

er, their fluidity and volatility make them unsuited to shaping public discourse or public space."[10]

Efficiency, instant communication in the briefest form possible, demands immediacy, which is to say the absence of mediation: through profiles, we mediate our presences, how, when, and where we choose. We are all called to be online 24/7, which the dawn of the smartphone has made viable. Total noise, total reaction, and total presence is the trinitarian god worshipped in the digital temple of Twitter today. "More and more, interfaces are being eliminated. Mediation and representation are viewed as a lack of transparency and inefficiency."[11] With the omnipresent eye of the smartphone, first-hand, unmediated accounts of nearly every event is now attainable and accessible.

In turn, immediacy compels conformity, as the real-time appearance of news stories, scandals, and viral content are shared constantly and instantly. Knowledge of new information is the new wisdom. The competent actor is the eternally present actor. An anonymous public interrogates us with updates, alerts, and live videos: what is your reaction; who are your allies; and who is to blame? To respond too late is to be irrelevant or complicit; to respond quickly is to attract the possibility of celebrity.

Might we begin to draw a distinction between mere information and knowledge? To return to the ancient philosophers, might there be some connec-

---

[10] Byung-Chul Han, *In the Swarm* (Cambridge, MA: MIT Press, 2017), 7.

[11] Han, 15.

tion between the conditions that form the faculty of judgment and the possibility of virtue? Is there such a thing as over-involvement? Might Hannah Arendt, and the long history of philosophy, be correct: does thought require a *distancing* from the immediacy of the present, from whatever composes the goings-on of the moment, for its vitality? When transparency and immediacy are the only virtues, what happens to the slow-to-come, the truth that develops over time, or the silence that seems essential for the act of thinking?

To suggest these questions today is to ignore, seemingly, the greatest advantage of our digital age: with the profusion of data as information, theories and trust are no longer required to understand ourselves or interact with others. Data mining has shown us that theories, the stuff of thought, are antiquated. Indeed, "inconceivably vast quantities of data have made theoretical models superfluous....hypothetical models are unnecessary. Directly comparing and balancing out data yields better results. Correlation takes the place of causality."[12] Everything is public, open to view. Because trust is bound to the unknown, the wisdom of our day declares it is no longer needed. Transparency is the rule. Trust is *obsolete*, and therefore compulsion rules much of what we now call social "conversations."

What, then, are we to make of the curious case of Jordan B. Peterson who makes *telling the truth*, and therefore, being *trustworthy*, central to his thought? Who, with the clumsiness of a person

---

12. Han, 78.

groping for things in the dark to orient himself, thinks aloud and, in real-time, revises, clarifies, and improves upon what he says? This man, who has spoken to over 150,000 people for his *12 Rules* book tour, lectured over 15 times on the Bible, amassing some 200,000 plus words on its behalf,[13] appears anachronistic. Many have been motivated to either denounce or praise him. Not only have staples of traditional news platforms and cultural commentary mediums like the *New York Times*,[14,15] *The Guardian*,[16] *The New York Times Review of Books*,[17] *Channel 4 News*,[18] and *NBC's 60*

---

[13] See transcripts on "Transcripts Archives," Jordan Peterson, https://jordanbpeterson.com/category/transcripts/.

[14] Jordan Peterson, "On the New York Times and "Enforced Monogamy," Jordan Peterson, June 08, 2018, accessed June 12, 2018, https://jordanbpeterson.com/media/on-the-new-york-times-and-enforced-monogamy/.

[15] David Fuller, "Jordan Peterson and the New York Times-a Rorschach Test for the New Culture Wars," Medium, May 19, 2018, accessed June 20, 2018, https://medium.com/rebel-wisdom/jordan-peterson-and-the-new-york-times-a-rorschach-test-for-the-culture-wars-3c172113b3d0.

[16] Taken from the now defunct *Knife Media* website: https://www.theknifemedia.com/world-news/spot-hit-piece-case-jordan-peterson/.

[17] Jordan B. Peterson, "Kwakwaka'wakw Controversy," Jordan Peterson, March 23, 2018, accessed March 30, 2018, https://jordanbpeterson.com/media/kwakwakawakw-controversy/.

Minutes[19] significantly mischaracterized his ideas—taking them out of context and placing them in the traditions of offensive and nefarious actors—but so have newer platforms like *Vox,*[20] *The Walrus,*[21] and *Vice.*[22] Yet, on the opposite side, *Quillette,* an online publication, recently skyrocketed in popularity as it published and continues to publish content related to identity politics, the reliability of tradi-

---

[18]Conor Friedersdorf, "Why Can't People Hear What Jordan Peterson Is Actually Saying?" The Atlantic, January 22, 2018, accessed February 03, 2018, https://www.theatlantic.com/politics/archive/2018/01/putting-monsterpaint-onjordan-peterson/550859/.

[19]Liberty Banner, "Ben Shapiro SLAMS NBC for Attacking Jordan Peterson(must Watch)," YouTube, April 30, 2018, accessed May 05, 2018, https://www.youtube.com/watch?time_continue=2&v=4AEzAePjSlE.

[20] Jordan B. Peterson, "Response to Vox "Feminist Philosopher" Dr. Kate Manne of Cornell," Jordan Peterson, June 08, 2018, accessed November 08, 2018, https://jordanbpeterson.com/uncategorized/response-to-vox-feminist-philosopher-dr-kate-manne-of-cornell/.

[21] Uri Harris, "In Defence of Jordan B. Peterson," Quillette, August 23, 2018, accessed August 24, 2018, https://quillette.com/2017/12/01/defence-jordan-b-peterson/.

[22] See an analysis of the editing techniques used in the Jordan Peterson interview here: Todoke, "Incredible Dishonest Cutting & Editing of Jordan Petersons Vice Interview," YouTube, February 23, 2018, accessed February 25, 2018, https://www.youtube.com/watch?v=DZrSrZpX5l8&feature=youtu.be.

tional media outlets, college campus protests, social justice, psychology, feminism, and communism: all topics you would find in a typical Peterson lecture. The topics with which he engages draws crowds because they are some of the most important of our time. This in one way accounts for the vitriol and love people appear to have for this thinker.

Although many come to his aid, it is difficult to imagine many of the hit pieces on Peterson gaining traction without the help of social media. Looking at current research, it should not be surprising. MIT recently published the largest study of its kind on the spread of misinformation on Twitter:

> The data comprise ~126,000 stories tweeted by ~3 million people more than 4.5 million times. We classified news as true or false using information from six independent fact-checking organizations that exhibited 95 to 98% agreement on the classifications. Falsehood diffused significantly farther, faster, deeper, and more broadly than the truth in all categories of information, and the effects were more pronounced for false political news than for false news about terrorism, natural disasters, science, urban legends, or financial information.[23]

---

[23] Soroush Vosoughi, Deb Roy, and Sinan Aral, "The Spread of True and False News Online," Science, March 09, 2018, accessed March 18, 2018, http://science.sciencemag.org/content/359/6380/1146.

Misinformation, as a social currency on platforms designed to propel engagement rather than honest discourse, is more valuable than concepts. As former vice-president for user growth at Facebook, Chamath Palihapitiya, has said, "The short-term, dopamine-driven feedback loops that we have created are destroying how society works. No civil discourse, no cooperation, misinformation, mistruth."[24]

I was once of the opinion that Albert Camus had correctly selected the myth that embodies the spirit of our times. Living after Nietzsche's pronouncement that God is dead and we have killed him, we are left to find meaning for our lives outside of the religious structures that for so long brought form and content to social conceptions of life as a whole. The most courageous thing we could do, I thought, was to, as Nietzsche once put it, transform a *thus it happened* to a *thus I willed it*, and, like Sisyphus, accept the tasks of life as gifts.

I no longer think this is the embodied myth of our time. We are rather closer to Icarus, children of a culture that has both created a technological maze that is impossible to escape and, by our kinship to it, made us complicit in its transgressions. By all ap-

---

[24]Julia Carrie Wong, "Former Facebook Executive: Social Media Is Ripping Society Apart," The Guardian, December 12, 2017, accessed January, 2, 2018,
https://www.theguardian.com/technology/2017/dec/11/facebook-former-executive-ripping-society-apart.
And see *Time's* in depth story for more information: Katy Steinmetz, "How Chamath Palihapitiya Wants to Disrupt Silicon Valley," Time, July 19, 2018,
http://time.com/5342756/chamath-palihapitiya/.

pearances, our culture has given us the means to escape our unjustified imprisonment: the free, unfettered wings of social media communication, a digital environment that promised unprecedented levels of cooperation and dialogue. But this environment is stimulating in a way culture could not have predicted; our pride and youth, in evolutionary terms, compels us to do foolish things. And just as we think we are most free, in rarefied air of partisan truth and tribal divisions, our means of salvation become our means of destruction. Our wings seem to have fallen apart, and, the waters are collapsing on top of us.

Perhaps all is not yet lost. Platforms like Patreon have opened up massive reserves of crowd-funding for thinkers and projects not bound to the oversight of corporations or traditional media networks. Similarly, as Peterson has noted recently: an evolution in audible content comparable to the revolution of text that occurred with the Gutenberg Press is underway. Thanks to podcasts and YouTube, no longer is literacy a barrier to entry for thinking about big issues, learning about history, politics, philosophy, or science, or dialoguing with educated elites about the meaning of things. The barrier to entry for conversation, before confined nearly exclusively to entrance into the academy, is now either a smartphone or an internet connection: two things that, for the average person in the West, is orders of magnitudes more accessible than the academy.

The comparison with the Gutenberg Press doesn't end there, however. Martin Luther famously leveraged the new technology to spread his ideas and disperse tracts and pamphlets among his networks, countering misinformation and censures released by the Catholic Church and educating his followers on topics that were before only available by admittance into prestigious Catholic institutions. Jordan Peterson, and others who make up the group now known as "The Intellectual Dark Web,"[25] have similarly leveraged the now very popular technologies of YouTube and podcasts to spread their messages, educating their listeners on topics before only confined to the spaces of the academy or pricey, library-use only books, and correcting the massive piles of misinformation published about them by traditional mass media networks. And, much like Martin Luther, Peterson's interpretation of Christianity is offensive to many traditional Christian interpreters, and his work stands as a corrective to liberal theologies that have been overly politicized.

With and without the aid of these new technologies, commentaries abound on the University of Toronto's clinical psychologist. Most attempt to construct a myth of the man, a compelling simplification that deems him either a savior or a demon. Others recently are more overt reflections on the failure of traditional media to report his views coherently or accurately.[26] Peterson came to public

---

[25] Bari Weiss and Damon Winter, "Meet the Renegades of the Intellectual Dark Web," The New York Times, May 08, 2018, accessed May 08, 2018, https://www.nytimes.com/2018/05/08/opinion/intellectual-dark-web.html.

[26] Paul Benedetti, "The Peterson Principle: Intellectual Complexity and Journalistic Incompetence," Quillette, August

consciousness first by releasing a somewhat philosophical series of YouTube videos reflecting on the imminent passing of bill C-16, then exploded in popularity after a 3-hour-long interview on *The Joe Rogan Experience* back in 2016. He has published over 100 articles in psychology,[27] and has written a large, nearly impenetrable book on myth and religion, called *Maps of Meaning*, relating them to the problem of group identity in politics back in 1999. A psychology professor for over 20 years, he once related that in a class he has been teaching on the Holocaust, his job was to convince students that they would have been Nazis.[28] For an academic career expanding decades, he has been studying the problem of suffering, its relation to politics, and how religious myths provide answers to these questions that do not entail, and in fact criticize, the creation of a perfect society based on ideological uniformity.

Many who rely on social media, and from it receive most of the information with which they orient themselves toward the world, are repelled by Peterson, believing he is some kind of self-help

---

23, 2018, accessed August 24, 2018, http://quillette.com/2018/02/15/the-peterson-principle-intellectual-complexity-and-journalistic-incompetence/.

[27]https://www.researchgate.net/profile/Jordan_Peterson2.

[28] Ramble, "Jordan B Peterson: You Probably Would Have Been a Nazi," YouTube, August 24, 2017, accessed November 10, 2017, https://www.youtube.com/watch?v=tVCAhGL0ohw.

guru,[29] popular only because he is an alt-right prophet and a popularizer of dubious positive-thinking psychology. Gaining a still larger audience after the publication of *12 Rules for Life: An Antidote to Chaos*, hit pieces that intentionally misquote, misinterpret, and generally misrepresent the views of a man that cannot be contained in a five-minute video clip or 500-word article are more prevalent than ever.[30] We have, as it were, circled the wagons, yet we are now just shooting in the dark, aiming at anything that moves.

I discovered Peterson through his initial interview with Rogan, and I was immediately captivated by his application of Darwinian mechanisms of selection to religious myths and his fascinating take on everything from politics to philosophy, from psychology to religion. Now that the man has been properly situated in our cultural moment, as others more interested in that narrative than myself have defended him against common misconceptions,[31] I would like to outline the basic concepts that ground Peterson's thought. Having more than 300 hours'

---

[29] This is true but not in the way normally intended. See Christian Chensvold's article for more: Christian Chensvold, "YouTube's New Father Figure," National Review, June 19, 2017, accessed June 25, 2018, https://www.nationalreview.com/2017/06/jordan-p-peterson-self-help-guru-father-figure/.

[30] Ira Wells, "The Professor of Piffle," The Walrus, November 27, 2017, accessed December 10, 2017, https://thewalrus.ca/the-professor-of-piffle/.

[31] Harris, "In Defence."

worth of lectures online makes Peterson's work a mountain so large that the climb seems impossible, save only for the fervent. Why listen to a man many have already labelled a charlatan, a self-help guru, or worse, an alt-right prophet? One reason is because most have not placed his popular teaching in the context of his own work. My goal is to introduce his ideas to the average person without requiring that they spend a few months of their life figuring out his basic premises. What judgment they may pass on him is no concern of mine; I simply aim to provide an introduction that allow these judgments to be informed.

2. PETERSON AND THE REVIVAL OF PRAGMATISM

"You find an empirical philosophy that is not religious enough, and a religious philosophy that is not empirical enough for your purpose."[32] *"You want a system that will combine both things, the scientific loyalty to facts and willingness to take account of them, the spirit of adaptation and accommodation, in short, but also the old confidence in human values and the resultant spontaneity, whether of the religious or of the romantic type."*[33] *"I offer the oddly-named thing pragmatism as a philosophy that can satisfy both kinds of demand. It can remain religious like the rationalisms, but at the same time, like the empiricisms, it can preserve the richest intimacy with facts."*[34]

"Human motives sharpen all our questions, human satisfactions lurk in all our answers, all our formulas have a human twist."

William James, *Pragmatism and Other Writings*[35]

---

[32] William James, *Pragmatism and Other Writings* (New York: Penguin Books, 2000), 12.

[33] James, 14.

[34] James, 20.

[35] James, 106

W hat has characterized our scientific era, with its sticking to the facts, is a general, cultural discourse that largely ignores the history of ideas or the critical examination of our own assumptions regarding topics passed around like viruses on social networking platforms. This is most evident in the general attitude toward religion. With our knowledge of the sciences, we say the "claims" of religion are ludicrous. And, in the absence of philosophy, we forget to ask whether what we call a "claim" belongs to religion in the first place. This latter observation might appear senseless to many, because all we need to solve problems of knowledge are the facts, and we will draw our conclusions where they self-evidently lead. Yet, this very attitude is *not suggested by the facts themselves*. Human inquiries are oftentimes confused, not only in the way facts are interpreted, but also in the questions we use to discover which facts are "relevant" to begin with.

As the West becomes more secular, and notions like free will, God, the self, and consciousness are emptied of their original significations (and significances), the perennial questions of philosophy that caused us to seek enlightenment may be forgotten once-and-for-all. We are of the belief that the darkness surrounding us can be illuminated without enlightenment. We just need the double-AA-powered flashlight of common sense plus fact: we have the eyes to see, we need only some technological innovation to unveil the walls of the cave. Our trajectory is a merging of scientific fact with common sense reasoning. The hope is that this will bring about an informed, rational populace. This seems to be the thrust of much that passes for philosophy today, particularly in America, where skepticism and free-thought, bearing no family resemblance to the great traditions of the Skeptics and Freethinkers of the past, have set the terms for the discussion of ideas in the general public.

What more can be said of religion? Common sense observation tells us that nobody rises from the dead, the skies are empty, and all books are written by human hands. Everything in our world happens according to the laws of nature, and everything that happens, therefore, can be imitated, reproduced, and understood, given enough time and energy.

When I enrolled in my first religious studies course, I didn't expect to discover, on the very first day, the abyss between the scholarship about and the lived experience of religion. In his opening lecture, my professor talked about the purpose of the class—to understand religious people better by learning about religious history and symbols. And immediately after we looked at polls from the Pew Research, so that we might have a baseline knowledge of religious demographics in America. The startling thing to me was, "the U.S. Religious Knowledge Survey shows that large numbers of Americans are uninformed about the tenets, practices, history and leading figures of major faith traditions – including their own."[36]

---

[36] Joseph Liu, "U.S. Religious Knowledge Survey," Pew Research Center's Religion & Public Life Project, December 19, 2017, accessed September 02, 2018,

This, of course, begs the question: how is it that we understand religious people better by learning about religious history, if it does not factor in to the lived experience of religious people? Is scholarship of religion, its objects dealing with cultural and historical symbols, artifacts, and texts, tantamount to the lived experience of religion, the content of which is lived experience itself?

There are many ways to fall down on this question. Some people, whom I will call "rationalists," think all belief is undergirded by assumptions, and that to make these assumptions explicit is to understand the meaning of a belief. Others, "empiricists" think beliefs serve functions in particular forms of life and communities. To understand the meaning of these beliefs is to understand the functions they play in the lives of believers within the contexts of their communities. There is yet a third way of thinking about this: the pragmatic way, where language itself, understood as a tool, contains the keys for the meaning of beliefs. Since language is conceived of as a tool of adaptation, to understand the meaning of beliefs is, therefore, to understand how they enable one to live and act within their environments. This last avenue I think is the best angle from which to understand Jordan Peterson's work regarding religion.

A remarkable amount of hot air has been generated over Jordan Peterson's use of the word "truth." Especially following his first appearance on Sam Harris' podcast, a large swath of people have pro-

---

http://www.pewforum.org/2010/09/28/u-s-religious-knowledge-survey/.

claimed that Peterson is redefining the term. Below, I want to outline how Peterson is indebted to William James by referring to William James' 1907 lecture, *Pragmatism*, which will set the stage for our later venture into his ideas concerning perception, meaning, religion, and politics. The debt is accrued not only in his use of the term "truth," and his method of inquiry, but much more.

William James' 1907 Lecture

Read today, it is astonishing how the intellectual scene of 1907 so closely resembles to our own. In *Pragmatism*, William James intended to offer a vision of philosophy—a method on one hand and a definition of truth on the other—which would not be susceptible to the criticisms rightly leveled against abstract rationalisms and would avoid the equally devastating shortcomings of reductive empiricisms. This should not escape our notice. As the modern return to reason and rationality in the secular world tends to simplify the picture of humans to complex machines, our politics, especially on the radical left, has dismissed truth altogether, reducing truth claims to power plays.

Reading James today, we might also notice his assessment of the contemporary intellectual stock of theory at his time: "Never were as many men of a decidedly empiricist proclivity in existence as there are at the present day."[37] Science has come of age, and it has displaced, in large part, our reliance on older ways of thinking. Evidence of this presents

---

[37] James, 12.

itself immediately. Just reflect for a moment on what "truth" might mean. In today's scientifically imbued world, we understand truth to mean "correspondence with reality," or perhaps "claims supported by facts." But there is a more general notion of truth, in fact older,[38] that is coming on the scene once more. Peterson revitalizes it, where James made it essential to his philosophical vision.

Below I offer James' alternative to rationalism and empiricism. He calls this "pragmatism." For the reader's benefit, in the sections on pragmatism below I will stay very close to James' text. After, I will offer commentary-heavy expositions concerning where Peterson has been influenced by pragmatism specifically, and how his conversations with the likes of Sam Harris proves this connection compelling for the modern intellectual landscape.

Theories as Instruments: The Method

To me, the most interesting thing about pragmatism is that it situates our language, and particularly our theories, within the natural world. Theories are not to be looked upon as expressions of eternal timeless truths, nor are they to be understood as mere descriptions of factual states of reality (although a subset of the total set of propositions called "theories" certainly are). The very nature of a theory is that it is instrumental: "all our theories are *instrumental*, are mental modes of *adaptation* to reality...."[39]

---

[38] Perhaps first used in Plato, this notion of truth understands it to be intrinsically connected to the good.

[39] James, 86 (emphasis his).

Because theories are *tools,* the pragmatic philosophical method aims to settle abstract disputes by looking at the consequences that beliefs have in the world. For pragmatists, "There can *be* no difference anywhere that doesn't *make* a difference elsewhere—no difference in abstract truth that doesn't express itself in a difference in concrete fact and in conduct consequent upon that fact, imposed on somebody, somehow, somewhere, and somewhen."[40] Pragmatism prevents theorizing from becoming an empty game, because it asks us to understand the very *meaning* of theories in light of how they lead to certain consequences over others: "to develop a thought's meaning, we need only determine what conduct it is fitted to produce: that conduct is for us its sole significance."[41]

Thus, the method of pragmatic philosophy entails making connections between what people believe the truth to be, the way in which those beliefs play out in their everyday lives, and how these beliefs function in relation to other truths already believed. Though seemingly banal, this method entails a different conception of how truths are arrived at than common sense would tell us. Pragmatism points out that rarely are truths recognized *as true* by processes of induction or deduction. Nor do tautologies compel us: the airtight logic of certain biblical fundamentalists, that the Bible is the Word of God because the Bible says it is the Word of God,

---

[40] James, 27 (emphasis his).

[41] James, 25.

though it may express the grammar of their rationality, does not convince anyone who is not already a believer. This is to say that the reasons we give for beliefs we understand to be true typically are not constitutive, but are rather descriptive, of our own lines of thinking. They do not have the *compelling force* of truth. Why? Because, as James says, our experiences, our other beliefs about what is true, our memories, and various other factors contribute to the *force* of truth. James describes the process with an analogy to how new opinions are formed:

> The individual has a stock of old opinions already, but he meets a new experience that puts them to a strain. Somebody contradicts them; or in a reflective moment he discovers that they contradict each other; or he hears of facts with which they are incompatible; or desires arise in him which they cease to satisfy. The result is an inward trouble to which his mind till then had been a stranger, and from which he seeks to escape by modifying his previous mass of opinions. He saves as much of it as he can, for in this matter of belief we are all extreme conservatives. So he tries to change first this opinion, and then that (for they resist change very variously), until at last some new idea comes up which he can graft upon the ancient stock with a minimum disturbance of the latter, some idea that mediates between the stock and the new experience and runs them into one another most felicitously and expediently.

This new idea is then adopted as the true one. It preserves the older stock of truths with a minimum of modification, stretching them just enough to make them admit the novelty, but conceiving in ways as familiar as the case leaves possible. An *outree* explanation, violating all our preconceptions, would never pass for a true account of a novelty. We should scratch round industriously till we found something less eccentric. The most violent revolutions in an individual's beliefs leave most of his older order standing. Time and space, cause and effect, nature and history, and one's own biography remain untouched. New truth is always a go-between, a smoother-over of transitions. It marries old opinion to new fact so as ever to show a minimum of jolt, a maximum of continuity. We hold a theory true just in proportion to its success in solving this 'problem of maxima and minima.' But success in solving this problem is eminently a matter of approximation. We say this theory solves it on a whole more satisfactorily than that theory; but that means more satisfactorily to ourselves, and individuals will emphasize their points of satisfaction differently.[42]

We learn from James that the beliefs we hold as true are first called into question when we hear contradictory beliefs, are questioned by others, assimilate new facts, accidently realize incompatibilities in our beliefs in moments of reflection, experience realities that cannot be sufficiently interpreted by

---

[42] James, 31.

our current beliefs, or, motivated by feeling, instinct, or desire, our beliefs prove dissonant with our living circumstances. What we do first is attempt to modify the troubled belief by isolating it from others, narrowing in on and revising the smallest portion of our overall view of the world as possible. With minimal disturbance, we come to recognize a new belief as true to the extent that it can mediate between old beliefs and novelty. "It makes itself true, gets itself classed as true, by the way it works; grafting itself then upon the ancient body of truth, which thus grows much as a tree grows by the activity of a new layer of cambium."[43] In its functional account of truth, pragmatism tells us that our theories, our truths, are tools for adapting to reality, marrying our old selves with an environment that demands us to adapt to its novel conditions. "The reasons why we call things true is the reason why they *are* true, for 'to be true' *means* only to perform this marriage-function."[44]

The Questions of Correspondence, Reality, and the Good

To some, this approach may, on the face of it, appear to be simple nonsense. Truth means for us that a belief corresponds to reality, that it has *factual* content. Without help from philosophy, science has situated us in a world of facts. Today we are so grounded in this world that the first mention of God, or free will, or the soul draws smirks and conde-

---

[43] James, 33.

[44] James, 33 (emphasis his).

scension. Claims about such beings or phenomena certainly do not correspond with anything known to the sciences. Pragmatism seems to be shifting the question of truth to the question of meaning, and these are seemingly two different conversations.

Yet, pragmatism in fact does not deny our factual, scientifically-described reality. It is firmly positioned within it. What pragmatism does is call into question what we mean by "correspondence to reality" and offers a naturalist account of this connection.

> But the great assumption of the intellectualists is that truth means essentially an inert static relation. When you've got your true idea of anything, there's an end of the matter. You're in possession; you *know*; you have fulfilled your thinking destiny. You are where you ought to be mentally; you have obeyed your categorical imperative; and nothing more need follow on that climax of your rational destiny....
>
> Pragmatism, on the other hand, asks its usual question. 'Grant an idea or belief to be true,' it says, 'what concrete difference will its being true make in any one's actual life? How will the truth be realized? What experience will be different from those which would obtain if the belief were false? What, in short, is the truth's cash-value in experiential terms?'
>
> The moment pragmatism asks this question, it sees the answer: *True ideas are those that we can assimilate, validate, corroborate and verify. False ideas are those that we can not.* That is

the practical difference it makes to us to have true ideas; that, therefore I, is the meaning of truth, for it is all truth is known-as.[45]

For James, the question of truth does not originate in an ethereal realm known as "the rational," where truth is merely an intellectual problem to be solved, much like algorithms in mathematics, according to laws of logic that are similar to laws of nature. Of course, logic will play some role. But logic does not compel us to ask the question of truth, it gives us a way of describing what we believe to be true. The question of truth arises in experience when a disjuncture exists between our stock of beliefs and our experience: when there is contradiction, incongruity, or a change of mood. In his naturalism, James believes truth has practical reasons for its existence.

We live in a world of realities that can be infinitely useful or infinitely harmful. Ideas that tell us which of them to expect count as the true ideas in all this primary sphere of verification, and the pursuit of such ideas is a primary human duty. The possession of truth, so far from being here an end in itself, is only a preliminary means towards other vital satisfactions.[46]

This, indeed, is what agreement with reality means:

---

[45] James, 88.
[46] James, 89.

To 'agree' in the widest sense with a reality *can only mean to be guided either straight up to it or into its surroundings, or to be put into such working touch with it as to handle either it or something connected with it better than if we disagreed*....And often agreement will only mean the negative fact that nothing contradictory from the quarter of that reality comes to interfere with the way in which our ideas guide us elsewhere.[47]

Many who have commented on Peterson's connection with pragmatism point to a somewhat caricatured definition: truth is anything that works. As if we can thereby gain all the relevant information from these simplified words, the common objection is put to pragmatism that "what works for one person doesn't work for another," and that pragmatism is therefore to be accounted among the failed theories of postmodernism. It appears to many that pragmatism gives a relativistic account of truth. But this is far from the case. Pragmatism escapes relativism by its appeal to reality as *that which must be accounted for* in our everyday lives. "All our truths are beliefs about 'Reality'; and in any particular belief the reality acts as something independent, as a thing *found*, not manufactured."[48]

---

[47] James, 93 (emphasis his).
[48] James, 107 (emphasis his).

Any idea that helps us to *deal*, whether practically or intellectually, with either the reality or its belongings, that doesn't entangle our progress in frustrations, that *fits*, in fact, and adapts our life to the reality's whole setting, will agree sufficiently to meet the requirement [of agreement, or 'correspondence' with reality]. It will hold true of that reality.[49]

For an idea *to work* does not mean that it makes us happy, induces sensations of pleasure, or merely coheres with previous beliefs. That which works is that which allows us to adapt to the reality that in every moment may change unpredictably:

We must find a theory that will *work*; and that means something extremely difficult; for our theory must mediate between all previous truths and certain new experiences. It must derange common sense and previous belief as little as possible, and it must lead to some sensible terminus or other that can be verified exactly. To 'work' means both these things; and the squeeze is so tight that there is little loose play for any hypothesis.[50]

For beliefs to have consequences they must have pay-off. To have beliefs that effectively adapt us to reality is to have beliefs that *pay*. For the per-

---

[49] James, 94. See the next chapter for a further explication of "reality," from Jordan Peterson's perspective.

[50] James, 95.

son who learns from reality that a snake's bite is poisonous and believes this to be true, a pragmatist would say the meaning of this truth is that the snake's bite must be avoided at all costs. The simple description of a snake's bite as poisonous and the further taxonomization of snake bites into categories of higher and lesser degrees of poison are parasitic on, and abstractions from, this primary notion of truth.[51]

To hold true beliefs is to have an evolutionary advantage over people who hold false beliefs. The person who believes the poisonous snake's bite is in fact a serum for the flu will not likely survive to pass these false beliefs, like genes, to offspring. For James, "It pays for our ideas to be validated. Our obligation to seek truth is part of our general obligation to do what pays. The payments true ideas bring are the sole why of our duty to follow them. Identical whys exist in the case of wealth and health."[52] And, furthermore:

> [T]ruth is *one species of good*, and not, as is usually supposed, a category distinct from good, and co-ordinate with it. *The true is the name of whatever proves itself to be good in the way of belief, and good, too, for definite, assignable reasons*. Surely you must admit this, that if there were *no* good for life in true ideas, or if the

---

[51] Next chapter we will explore Peterson's notion of the primary conception of the world as a forum for action. This is a very similar idea.

[52] James, 101.

knowledge of them were positively disadvanta-geous and false ideas the only useful ones, then the current notion that truth is divine and pre-cious, and its pursuit a duty, could never have grown up or become a dogma. In a world like that, our duty would be to *shun* truth, rather. But in this world…certain ideas are not only agreea-ble to think about, or aggregable as supporting other ideas that we are fond of, but they are also helpful in life's practical struggles.[53]

We have gathered from William James' prag-matism that functionally a belief is true to the extent that it enables us to adapt to reality. This entails that truth is fundamentally concerned with actions: those actions best adapted to reality.54 What follows is that truth is embedded in a motivational framework: a framework of good and bad. We must ask now what the connection between the true and the good is.

"What would be better for us to believe"! This sounds very like a definition of truth. It comes very near to saying "what we *ought* to believe": and in *that* definition none of you would find any oddity. Ought we ever not to believe what it is *better for us* to believe? And can we then

---

[53] James, 38.

[54] We will explore more in depth what the notion of reali-ty means in the coming chapters. Essentially it involves not only the objects of natures, climate, the pressures of natural selection, but also our social reality, group expectations, tradi-tions, and individual survival.

keep the notion of what is better for us, and what is true for us, permanently apart?

Pragmatism says no, and I fully agree with her.[55]

Daniel Dennett, a philosopher indebted to the tradition of pragmatism, agrees with James that we can derive ought from an is by positing the origin of this distinction in nature (i.e., evolutionary theory). We can understand the notions of (1) "good" and (2) "bad" as coming from (1) the survival and, at times, flourishing following from adaptive behavior and (2) the punishment or death that followed maladaptive behavior.[56] Indeed, the consequences of behavior—life or death, or reward or punishment—readily bring to mind the language of morality. We might say, with Peterson, that the truth of a belief is necessarily embedded in a larger framework, where we find that highest principle is *that which serves life*. Though I only pointed to it here, the good and the true can be connected in the common framework of motivational behavior. More will be said on this as we turn to the discussion Jordan Peterson had with Sam Harris concerning the nature of truth.

Before we begin, it will be helpful to reiterate the importance of the pragmatic notion of truth by briefly situating it in relation to the traditionally epistemological account. The theory of truth pragmatism gives should not be seen as *opposing* epis-

---

[55] James, 38
.

[56] http://ase.tufts.edu/cogstud/dennett/papers/Brandom.pd f

temological notions of truth. Whereas epistemological concepts of truth attempt to give an account of what in the form or nature of propositions make claims true, or, to put it another way, under what conditions a claim can be asserted justifiably as true, the pragmatism account is a *functional* account. Where the former class of concepts are normative, the latter are descriptive.

The pragmatist account describes how we might achieve the kind of truths epistemology tells us are attainable: how we come to perceive truth in the natural world in the first place. For example, to know what conditions must obtain for a bishop to move diagonally on a chess board, and therefore to say, "it is true that a bishop moves diagonally on a chess board," is to occupy the appropriate epistemological space to justifiably make the claim about bishops. This is akin to the epistemological notion of truth. However, this account does not preclude the functional account that might follow; it presupposes it. To describe how one learns to play chess, to understand strategy, to place "chess" within the class of objects known as "games," to have the temperament that makes game-playing with others a likelihood, to live in a socio-economic environment that promotes the playing of chess, and so on, is to give a functional account of the origin of the truth that "a bishop moves diagonally on a chess board." These two accounts belong together. Where one focus on the theory of a claim, the latter focuses on the reality of a claim: the real conditions that make the claim sensible and possible.

To say that the truth is what corresponds to reality, as in a more conventional epistemological account, tells us in no way how it is we come to know something as true, what correspondence means in the lives of people or the context of the communities in which they live, or what mechanisms of belief or perception make the question of truth relevant in the first place. This is what pragmatism attempts to describe, and so it is a categorical error to oppose it to the correspondence theory of truth.

The Question of Truth with Sam Harris[57]

Now that we have briefly outlined William James' concept of truth, we can readily see that Peterson takes the pragmatic notion of truth and houses it in a Darwinian framework. In the now notorious discussion about truth on the *Waking Up Podcast* with Sam Harris, Peterson says our epistemological situation, the boundaries of which create the conditions for belief, is not bounded by eternal, timeless restrictions of logic, nor is it guided by an objective rational motif existing somewhere behind or beyond the world, if by rational motif we mean the discovery of truths that exist independent of human experience. Our epistemological situation has been determined by nature, as Darwin discovered. This meant for him that the ever-changing environment precluded the possibility of a stable, unchanging relationship to it. Organisms not having

---

[57] The exposition below acts as both a summary and commentary of Peterson's conversation with Sam Harris on *The Waking Up Podcast #62 – What is True? (with Jordan B. Peterson)*.

the resources within themselves to always adapt sufficiently to their continually transforming environments had to rely on random variance to yield novel traits that would allow sufficient adaptation. Those whose traits were beneficial, survived, and propagated, and then the cycle of life began again, with environmental change, random variance, death or survival and propagation. Our epistemic situation is delineated by unpredictable change, requiring adaptation to account for new information and environmental stimuli. We can see with James, the same happens to our beliefs.

Consequently, Peterson thinks all truth claims must be located within this natural process. This means that all intellectual endeavors are housed within the behavioral framework of adaptation to the environment, which implies an ethic. If truth is understood as "efficiency toward obtaining an aim," then the aim places a demand on action, namely, the achievement of the aim. All aims, Peterson believes, are ultimately motivated by what serves life, because evolution is about the evolution of life. Before we make our beliefs abstract and codified, we embody them, creating motivational frameworks that ground our convictions and desires. The ultimate motivational framework, Peterson thinks, values *that which serves life* as the highest principle. This allows him to make the claim that if, for instance, science basically conceptualizes the world as composed of subatomic particles, and through science we succeed in the creation of the atom bomb, and this creation ends human life, or all life, as we know it, then the truth of the proposition that the world is fundamentally composed of subatomic atoms was not *sufficiently* true, and perhaps for what it left out: the surrounding context of life. He thinks our view of the world today may be fundamentally flawed, and that we cannot take this for granted, for science has made us strip the world of affect, isolating objects in the world from us and from their consequences for life.58

In the conversation, Sam Harris initially characterizes Peterson's view by referring back to his own professor, Richard Rorty. Harris gives his initial overview of Rorty, a leader of modern pragmatism, in the following way: Rorty thought pragmatism boiled down to the claim that we can never stand outside human conversation and talk about reality or truth as they are within themselves. We never come into contact with naked truth, all we have is our conversation. The currency of truth is what successfully passes in a conversation about truth. All we have is the ever-expanding horizon line of successful conversation. But, Peterson doesn't like this characterization and thinks it is too close to postmodernism.

After concurring with him on this point, it is odd that Harris then attributes this position to Peterson himself.59 Sam Harris, in rebuttal to Peterson's con-

---

58 A description of this is in the next chapter.

59 This, I think, is the main cause of the 2-hour sluggish discussion about where, in fact, they disagreed. They were not explicitly disagreeing on much. Harris seemed to be attributing his original view of pragmatism, derived from his professor Richard Rorty, to Peterson, and not taking Peterson's position with its unique solutions and challenges. Peterson can, as has been shown, accept that there is a reality outside

ceptualization of truth, wants to oppose realism to pragmatism. The core tenet of realism is that it is possible for everyone to be mistaken about the truth, that there can be a consensus around truth but it is possible for the consensus to be wrong, and that there is a horizon of cognition beyond which we cannot see and about which we could be wrong about at the moment. Sam Harris, here, unwittingly it seems, confers Rorty's position to Peterson, as he claims that the pragmatist cannot posit an independent reality outside human conversation. The pragmatist can only place it within current conversation, equivocating truth with what works for us at the moment. Harris thinks there is no larger context of truth claims that situates the pragmatist conception of truth in a broader sphere where we can say something, and perhaps everything, is wrong with what people currently believe, though the beliefs may be useful for the time-being.

This is, as we have shown, inaccurate. The entire *pay-off* for truth is that it enables us to adapt to our environments, to the fact that we live with other people, and to our own inner musings, interpretations, beliefs, and desires. Indeed, as we will see with the realm of order and the tyrannical father, there is a motivational framework which assumes it knows everything there is to know about truth but cannot, in fact, adapt to the dawning, novel future. This has deadly consequences. There are some truths that are not *true enough* to allow us to thrive in the future. This healthy skepticism as to what we

conversation. This is a position William James takes himself in his lectures on pragmatism.

believe to be true is indeed a vital part of pragmatism. Reality, that which selects and to which we must adapt, is the ultimate arbiter of truth claims.

Yet, Sam Harris also worries that if we take pragmatism seriously, it would entail that we couldn't verify a truth claim until the end of time, because we will never know what serves human life ultimately. This need not bother us, for this is always the case: even with reductive correspondence theories of truth. It didn't bother Newtonian physicists that what they took to be true could only be falsified, and therefore never verified. Yet progress of a kind was achieved. And this is the case for all science. No theory of truth will ever solve this problem and this is not what is at stake in the conversation. As William James says, "We have to live to-day by what truth we can get to-day, and be ready to-morrow to call it falsehood."[60] What is at stake is what our fact-seeking, truth-perceiving attitudes and behaviors are about. And the answer for James and Peterson is survival, whereas for Sam Harris, it is the accumulation of true descriptions, or facts, about the world.

For Peterson, the method of the sciences, and the reduction of truth to fact, may be like the linguistic version of a disease. As it makes truth about disembodied objects, it forgets the natural framework in which it is actually housed. To gather facts we have to reduce and exclude, to strip motivational significance from objects in the world.[61] It forgets that some things work within the confines of the

---

[60] James, 98.

[61] More on this in the next chapter.

rules of an experiment, but not in the real world. To generalize from the facts discovered within the controlled conditions of laboratories can lead to catastrophic consequences in the real world. This indicates to Peterson that science operates not according to the most general, or "ultimate" conception, of truth, but one parasitic upon it. For the ultimate truth is that which serves life. Although Harris agrees that the scientific endeavor must be housed within a moral endeavor, he does not agree with Peterson that this entails the scientific notion of truth must be subjected to a moral framework. This is the disagreement they danced around the entire conversation.

In conclusion, for Peterson the Darwinian notion of truth is one of *moral* truth, and these are the truths that are the highest, around which all facts should be gathered and interpreted, and all human endeavors understood. "It means technically that the only final way of sorting out whether a scientific claim is sufficiently true is through Darwinian means. Because I think the Darwinian process is the only way of adjudicating truth."

Note on Two Objections

So let us take for granted that Peterson is correct that the Darwinian process is the only way to adjudicate truth. Sam Harris has raised the objection that we cannot, still, decide between equally-useable truths. Similarly, Brett Weinstein has objected that, because different religions have different motivational frameworks, it appears that we should place science at the top of the hierarchy of truths because it has one thing religious frameworks don't: the ability to describe and categorize disparate systems of thought. I believe this is the furthest the conversation has gotten at this point, and it is difficult to imagine what answers may lie beyond this impasse.

Yet, it does seem as though we have to house our human endeavors, especially the search for truth, within the larger framework of human life and flourishing. There are facts about how to build 3D guns, but it does not follow that it is good for everyone to know these facts. There are some things worth knowing, others not so much. So what happens when disparate systems come into conflict, to Harris' point; or when different conceptions of *what serves life* compete with each other, to Weinstein's objection? I think we are seeing this right now, as it plays out in politics, the humanities, and the sciences. I think we have never escaped this problem: for truth is not a proposition that terminates the intellectual life, nor is it an eternal object which can stabilize our environments. Following James and Peterson, I think truth allows us to sufficiently adapt to our present environment, but it may need altering in light of conflicts and future knowledge.

The question of how best to conceptualize truth and reality is, indeed, in part a question about the ultimate grounding of human motivations, and Sam Harris and Brett Weinstein appear to have come to different conclusions regarding this issue. The fortuitous situation in which we find ourselves, however, is that despite the fact that fundamental points of view are coming into conflict, they are doing so over longform discussion on podcasts and stages.

They are democratic. They are based on some of the best ideas from different traditions of thought. Bad ideas are dying, better ideas are coming into focus. We are not killing each other over these differences. And, perhaps to Peterson's point, this might be because we have assumed the metaphysical superstructure of Christian myth to undergird our motivations: we have elevated spoken truth as a paramount virtue, and therefore honesty and civility as the appropriate motivational framework for these discussions. We have placed the individual at the center of discourse, without equating the individual with the infinite number of groups it is possible to classify the individual with. And we have determined that the best way to live is to speak the truth, without subsuming the value of truth to what negative reactions detractors may have. We have to keep ourselves honest, or else in in high stakes situations we will not be able to trust ourselves. If we take the idea seriously that beliefs are embodied before they are abstracted, it is possible that as a result we are all embodying the same game, in this circumstance, yet speaking about the rules differently. This can terminate our game only if our abstractions are then adopted as the essential aspect of the belief, and used to guide our political, moral, and philosophical games in the future. We must be very careful, therefore, how we speak, and to which truths we regard ourselves beholden.

That Peterson understands ideas to be embodied before they are abstracted into beliefs is significant here. For to agree with Peterson that our ideas do assume a metaphysical superstructure is just to say that there is a logic to our motivations. Turning to the next chapter, we will see how this logic, composing the grammar of stories, originated in myth. This is not tantamount to accepting Catholicism or Protestantism. Nor is it to say we need to return to pre-Reformation Christendom. We can take our cue from Peterson: what this means is we pay attention to the stories of the past to understand how they have constructed the present we find ourselves in. Then, and only then, might we have the tools with which to create a novel order of the present, as the unimaginable future confronts us with new challenges. Flushing out this claim more will be our focus in the rest of the book. As James wrote over 100 years ago:

> My thesis now is this, that *our fundamental ways of thinking about things are discoveries of exceedingly remote ancestors, which have been able to preserve themselves throughout the experience of all subsequent time.* They form one stage of equilibrium in the human mind's development, the stage of *common sense.* Other stage have grafted themselves upon this stage, but have never succeeded in displacing it.[62]

Conclusion

As we have seen, Jordan Peterson is heavily indebted to William James' philosophical pragmatism. Not only does this help explain Peterson's understanding of truth, but it also helps us understand

---

[62] James, 76 (emphasis his).

his fascination with religious ideas: ideas that, until recently, have been scorned and caricatured by secular thinkers. As James explained, "On pragmatic principles we cannot reject any hypothesis if consequences useful to life flow from it."[63] He wants us to think about not just what collection of facts we can discover through the methods of the sciences, or the theories we might construct with clever thought experiments, but also the very real consequences these human endeavors have for our world, ourselves, and others. To be a pragmatist is to scrutinize truth in light of its place in the real world. If in no other way, let us follow Peterson's lead in this undertaking.

---

[63] James, 119.

3. OUR MAPS OF MEANING: MYTH, SCIENCE, AND HIERARCHY

"Man is an animal, from the objective view-point, worthy of no more consideration than the opinion and opportunities of the moment dictate. From the mythic viewpoint, however, every individual is unique—is a new set of experiences, a new universe; has been granted the ability to bring something new into being; is capable of participating in the act of creation itself. It is the expression of this capacity for creative action that makes the tragic conditions of life tolerable, bearable— remarkable, miraculous."

Jordan Peterson, *Maps of Meaning* [64]

N ow that we have seen Peterson in light of William James, we will dig a bit deeper into his understanding of reality and the idea that our beliefs, and our truths, are housed within a motivational framework. Moving from William James, we will see also the influence of Carl Jung on Peterson's thought. Below, I want to outline how Peterson understands the relation between science and religion, and the roles that the conscious and

---

[64] Jordan B. Peterson, *Maps of Meaning: The Architecture of Belief* (London: Routledge, 1999), 467.

unconscious play in our interaction within the world. What is at stake might not be immediately apparent. Many in the West today are finding religion to be nonsensical, given its ostensibly and, genuinely at times, absurd beliefs, doctrines, and rituals. A popular view of religion, espoused recently by the "Four Horsemen" of atheism and those who came after,[65] is that in the development of human history religion was something like an early form of science, and religious beliefs in the supernatural were early attempts at understanding and controlling the world around us. Looking on rituals of the past, the view concludes rain dances were about rituals that attempted to cause rain, and, looking around today, sees a less primitive form of this ritual when people pray for God's healing. What use is religion, we are asked, if we now know the *true* causes of things in the universe?

Many have raised objections to this perspective,[66] and Peterson can be counted among them. For Peterson, science separates what religion brings together. Religion, as it understands the world by references to personalities and intentions, is logically distinct from the method of the sciences, which attempts to separate human perceptions and beliefs from the causes and effects of objects. Furthermore,

---

[65]https://en.wikipedia.org/wiki/New_Atheism#The_%22 Four_Horsemen%22.

[66] My favorite objection is raised by the philosopher Ludwig Wittgenstein in Remarks on Frazer's "Golden Bough." More objections can be found in Mircea Eliade's work, the philosopher of religion D. Z. Phillips, and religious scholars like Karen Armstrong.

Peterson does not think that people participated in religious traditions to discern the causes of things in a pre-scientific way, but rather to play out, in the forms of myths and rituals, the inner psychological workings of humanity, before humanity knew what psychology was. This idea helps us understand religious beliefs even today. As suggested by D. Z. Phillips, people who pray that God's will would be done in difficult times are not trying to control what happens, nor are they attempting to relinquish their own responsibility for events they are in control of. Rather, prayers like these are existentially orienting activities and have an approximate meaning of, "Come what may, I must be okay with what happens."[67] This interpretation can also apply to people who pray for healing. A religious perspective, far from trying to control the world, might actually be about coming to terms with it, and learning what it is to be human in the midst of change, unpredictability, and the sometimes arbitrary behaviors of other people. Connecting beliefs with how they change and direct lives, Peterson lays out the groundwork for understanding religion pragmatically.

The Ground of Perception

How we map meaning onto the world and ourselves is not entirely self-evident, Peterson says. He refers us, here, to a problem Daniel Dennett has written eloquently about: The Frame Problem in

---

[67] See D. Z. Phillip's *The Problem of Evil and the Problem of God.*

AI.[68] In short, the problem is that there are an infinite number of ways to interpret anything. How do we go about perceiving any thing as a thing? What constraints constitute the structures by which perception itself becomes possible?

It is enticing to think that we simply do see a world of objects, and that the only problem of perception is to understand how these objects work in the causal nexus. To loosen this bewitchment of language, think about how you might perceive your car. You drive it everyday, you know what the steering wheel does, how to brake, when it needs gas, the people to take it to for oil changes, etc. You think you know what it is. But now imagine driving on a backroad, in an unfamiliar town, at night, and your car breaks down. Now what do you "know" about your car? The problem that caused the breakdown, certainly, is to be located in the causal nexus, and a well-trained mechanic could find the issue and fix it, most likely. But how do you perceive your car now? Perhaps it is a shelter from the unfamiliar, or a symbol for all the things that have gone wrong with your day. This way of perception is much closer to how we perceive things in the everyday world, Peterson thinks.

About ten years ago I walked a small-town country road to get to a field where I would split wood for work that day. It was only about a three-mile walk, but I was carrying a backpack full of water, some tools, the head-end of a maul, and wearing steel-toe boots. I was weighed down, to say the

---

[68]http://www.idi.ntnu.no/~gamback/teaching/TDT4138/dennett84.pdf.

least. After walking for about two miles, I suddenly heard barking behind me. When I turned, I saw a huge dog running across a yard toward me. I looked around, and all I could see was a fence, cornfields, and a few large trees nearby. I darted for the trees, though, after a few steps realized I would not be quick enough to climb the tree before the dog chewed me to pieces. Stopping for a moment, trying to find some courage, I turned around and faced the dog and, in the deepest, loudest voice I could muster, yelled, "Go!" and pointed toward its home. Luckily, it stopped running immediately, and remained in its yard, although still barking from the property line. When I was in that moment, I scanned the environment, not to look for "objects," which is to say self-contained spatial entities with discernable traits, but I looked for "things-to-climb." Our primary mode of perception has to do with discerning things in the environment we can *use*: with our hands, ears, eyes, and the like. After this encounter, I was shaky with adrenaline for about half an hour, and I can remember that the rest of the walk to the worksite I was scanning the sides of the roads for possible places to position myself should another dog appear.

Peterson posits that our bodies function as a constraint on interpretation: we do not primarily view the world as a field of objects, but rather as a forum for action. And what is primary in our conception of the world are not things or objects, but rather tools and obstacles. To know the meaning of a thing is to know how it relates to us and our aims: to know its functional significance. The meaning of a "home," for instance, is "a place to live with loved ones." Consequently, the ways in which things affect us tend to be identified with the things themselves. When we feel fear about encountering a dog on a country road, we also identify the dog as a *thing to be feared*, which primes the brain to think of certain words and the body to react in certain ways.[69]

This is the level of perception in which religion is best understood. The functional significance of things is not separated from their meaning or value in our everyday lives. When somebody carries the photos of loved ones with them, maybe in their wallets, purses, or on phones, they do not believe they *literally* carry their loved ones with them, although these photos do symbolize their presence in some way. And perhaps the mere fact that they look at, or think about, these photos occasionally changes their actions and thoughts. This phenomenon can be used as an analogy for the Eucharist in the Christian church: taking of the bread and wine and calling them the body of Christ for some interpreters can be understood as a ritualized form of carrying photos of loved ones. Of course, there is much more going on than this. But this simple connection suggests a way in which a functional analysis of religion, like Peterson is doing, can proceed.

This may seem counterintuitive at first. The tradition of the West, where the language and concepts of science saturate our cultural landscape, has taught us to think of ourselves as bodies in motion,

---

[69] See the excellent book *Thinking Fast and Slow* by Daniel Kahneman.

our bodies as objects among other objects acting, reacting, and influencing other objects. After all, the laws of physics, and the biological mechanisms that make life possible, indeed reduce reality to simple entities interacting with one another, forming systems and ecosystems. There is nothing inherently *inaccurate* about this understanding of the universe. The only problem is that this kind of thinking is a *higher order* of thinking than the kind of thinking that occurs when we are shocked by the moment, when we find ourselves in a situation we know nothing about with things and people around us we know nothing of, or when we, like automatons, are just going through the motions of our routines.

A reason why the framing problem came about in AI is because computers are something like brains in vats; they are disembodied. Precisely the ostensible strength of common conceptions of AI—its lack of physical limitation—is perhaps its undermining weakness at this point. Peterson wants to bring us back to the relevance of our physical circumstances as embodied persons and how our ideas and ideals evolved from this fact, science included.

Religion and Science, the Conscious and the Unconscious

Yet, ironically, the fact that science is a second-order level of thinking is its strength on some level. Its great feat consists in stripping our functional interpretations from objects.[70] Galvanizing the Enlightenment, as it dispensed with religious doctrine

---

[70] Peterson, *Maps of Meaning*, 4.

as necessary for understanding the world of objects, science ensured the West amassed commodities and propelled innovation to previously unimaginable heights. This also has had some unintended consequences. What happens when the concepts we abstracted from our primary level of perceptions are developed in an abstract realm, and we begin to interpret ourselves, others, and the world with these artificial schemas?

To state the relationship between science and religion differently, the unconscious, where the depth of religion operates, is about the nervous system that connects everything together, where the conscious, where science works, deals with separation and the surface qualities of the external.[71] Unwittingly, the scientism of the secular critiques of religion has resurfaced a perennial problem in a particularly intense way: when consciousness looks upon itself as an object of experience, it is susceptible to separating itself from the unconscious, which harbors motivating drives that compel action in the first place. When this occurs, we fall prey to lurking pathologies. Attributing all the motivation and meaning of behavior to surface level causes like beliefs or rationality risks turning us into something like the cyclops, where one faculty is overdeveloped at the expense of all else.[72]

---

[71] C. G. Jung, *The Archetypes and the Collective Unconscious*, ed. R. F. C. Hull (Princeton, NJ: Princeton University Press, 1990), 19.

[72] Peterson makes this criticism of intellectuals in PowerfulJRE, "Joe Rogan Experience #958 - Jordan Peterson,"

Daniel Dennett has noted that philosophers are particularly adept at reprogramming their intuitions with thought experiments and logic.[73] Similarly, much of the appeal of Ludwig Wittgenstein's work lies in its criticisms of the ways in which philosophers take language from their ordinary contexts and place them into logical structures, stripping concepts and sentences of their meanings. The very fact that nobody, as Albert Camus noted, has given their life for the ontological argument is significant: the logical structures we use to talk about and conceptualize the world, ourselves, and others are *not* indeed equal to the world, ourselves, and others. A perfectly logical and coherent argument can be made for just about anything under the sun, but it will not mean that it is useful, or that it represents anything that actually exists, or that it *explains* anything. This may indeed be why hardly anyone is persuaded to become a Christian by hearing the arguments from philosophy of religion. Reason, of course, has its place, and I am not criticizing its use. But it is only one tool. Like the ears, eyes, hands, and mouth, it has limits and selects for only certain kinds of data points for its interpretations of reality. My point is simply that, like the old saying goes, if our only tool is a hammer, everything begins to look like a nail.

YouTube, May 09, 2017, accessed May 09, 2017, https://www.youtube.com/watch?v=USg3NR76XpQ.

[73] *Intuition Pumps and Other Tools for Thinking* by Daniel Dennett.

The unconscious is constituted by forms called archetypes, which are defined by Jung as something like "patterns of instinctual behavior;"[74] repressing or suppressing these drives leads to rationalizing behavior that, on a deep level, are yet still motivated by these unknown, instinctual forces. "There is no lunacy people under the domination of an archetype will not fall prey to."[75] We can distinguish between rationalizing behavior, which involves the use of reason to articulate the meaning of behavior *after the fact*, and reasonable behavior, which is composed of actions we take for certain reasons established beforehand. The fact that we are so often motivated by biological drives like hunger or fear, social goods like commodities or recognition, or psychological functions like meaning or identity, means that when we separate our drives from our behaviors, we can fall into rationalizing everything. We think we are in control of our actions, but we are not.

I came from a very dysfunctional family where communication with my siblings usually involved manipulation, and communication with my mom mainly involved her catastrophizing whatever illness she had seen on a commercial and then attributing it to herself (doctors could never find these illnesses when she went for checkups). After going to therapy for a while, I learned that as a form of psychological defense I had become desensitized from my emotions. The first time I was really away

---

[74] Jung, 44.

[75] Jung, 48.

from my family was while I was in college. My freshman year I had picked up what I could on Stoicism and took it to heart. The dictums to not try to control what is outside one's control and that attachment to things causes suffering, and so should be avoided, seemed deeply true to me, and I tried to embody these beliefs to live a better life. Little did I know, as rational and as effective as these beliefs are at limiting suffering, they reinforced my desensitization. I, of course, didn't know this at the time, but the reasonable schema of Stoicism was reinforcing psychological dysfunctions I had yet to recognize or deal with. I was rationalizing my disfunction. What was causing dysfunction in my family was in part that nobody tried to relate to each other as people, with emotions and all, but only in manipulative ways, as means toward ends. You can imagine how dissociation toward my siblings who I could not control exacerbated the disfunction. I no longer had to worry about their demands on me as *people*. Their desires, plans, and feelings became nonfactors in my Stoic world. Sometimes rationality masks unclean spirits.

One of Peterson's central notions is that "Ideas are embodied before they are abstract, and abstracted as a drama first."[76] This means, in part, that something like a system of Stoicism is not sufficient in itself to give us an ethic to live by, for motivational frameworks are always larger than any given motivational viewpoint. Society cannot be directly led by the concept of good to a good world, howev-

---

[76] JRE #958.

er good the world is conceived, because we are motivated by more than merely rational forces. We are motivated by unconscious forces and forms that manifest themselves in our actions. Of course, we can recognize them in our actions, but only when we have understood their patterns, and we do this by telling stories. This is what he means when he says ideas are abstracted as drama first. Because we pay attention to ourselves and tell stories, *we* are the subject of our stories, and those unconscious forms establish the grammar of these stories we tell. We might say, here, that, whereas science systematizes the separation of functional significance from objects, religion systematizes functional significance until everything comes under its purview.

These unconscious forms in which the automatic attribution of meaning to things occurs is codified in myth and narrative, which are instantiated in religion. The structures of religious myth produce an explicit logic that undergirds cultural hierarchies and religious traditions: "A religion is a set of stories that comes very close to the grammar of stories. They aren't stories you can dispense with."[77] Carl Jung thought that myths did not aim to explain the world, as in how the rain falls or how the position of the stars relate to the earth, but rather operated within the affective identification of objects with the self: myths are projections of the inner unconscious drama.

---

[77] Russell Brand, "Russell Brand & Jordan Peterson - Kindness VS Power | Under The Skin #46," YouTube, February 15, 2018, accessed February 15, 2018, https://www.youtube.com/watch?v=kL61yQgdWeM.

This, on the face of it, draws a line between the world of myth and the world of science. Said again: myth articulates the world from the point of view of interconnectedness, from the unconscious archetypes that motivate our actions and beliefs, and understands the world as a forum for action; science makes distinct what is interconnected with human motivations, and articulates things as they are apart from human action, as they are located within a world not bound to human beliefs.

For some of you, it may seem like Peterson has sidestepped, still, the problem of religious belief. It is all good and well if religion is a different order of thinking, if it reveals something about the forms of human psychology. But how can we know that? Isn't it just simply the case that religion, especially Christian fundamentalism, attempts to explain the world as science does, as noted in its doctrine of creationism or intelligent design? Evolution is called into question by Christians every day in America. Indeed, the Creation Museum has made a business out of it. There seems to be no basis to know that religion really operates in this way, and that our functional interpretations of religion really are useful, and not, in fact, just reflections of beliefs secularism produced.

The problem of the relation between myth and science is complex, and, as indicated by Peterson when he recognized it, seemingly inescapable. Science and religion appear to be in conflict, and as science increases its knowledge, the mythic structures of religion must be left behind. Why would we, for instance, choose to live, once again, before the Enlightenment, when religious wars dominated Europe, and all claims to truth were bound to the doctrines of institutions that could interpret these doctrines according to their own self-serving ends? Yet, "If the religious realm and the scientific realm exist, they have to be unifiable at some point."[78] For Peterson, this connection consists in the grounding of the archetypes of the collective unconscious in Darwinian evolution.

Archetypes and Darwin

If it is true that the world is conceptualized best as primarily a forum for action, then what counts as our environment, in terms of Darwinian structures of adaptation, does not entirely, or even necessarily, associate adaptive traits to the objects of the world, but at least also to the tools that enable us to live and thrive in multiple environments among multiple groups of people. Our environment, in evolutionary terms, is not only natural, adhering to processes of cause and effect in nature, but also social and technological, providing the aims and means that achieve sustainable social relations with other people.

Now we enter the realm of hierarchy. I have heard Peterson explain the development of hierarchies in two ways. Here, I will focus on sexual selection, as the first time I heard Peterson describe the development of hierarchy he used this analysis to do so. Later, a more generally philosophical argument for the development of hierarchy will be

---

[78] UTS #46.

used. On the face of it, it does not appear that these two explanations are contradictory or mutually exclusive, but the differences in detail are significant and point to different forms of inquiry. Perhaps this is why he gave the exposition below in reference to religion and the later in reference to politics. I think both formulations are interesting to consider in their own right and therefore include both, but in their appropriate sections.[79]

Grounding our social aims for success, recognition, and commodities is an enduring motivator of action: one very important thing that separates us from chimps is that the females of our species select for sexual reproduction, and the traits exhibited particularly by brute males are not regularly selected for.[80] The selective mechanisms of females qualify what count as good aims and bad aims, and therefore the beliefs and character traits that are functionally relevant or "good" increase the probability of reproduction and those that are functionally useless or "bad" decrease the probability of reproduction. These aims and traits form into hierarchies of competence,[81] which act as "a distributive computa-

---

[79] See chapter 6 for Peterson's other explanation of hierarchy.

[80] Yet even in chimps, it is not the brute that gets sexual dominance, Peterson has said, because if the brute has an off day, then two beta males will tear him from limb to limb: it is better, at least, even in chimp communities, to be tolerant and cooperative than to merely be a brute.

[81] Recently Peterson has been using this phraseology instead of "dominance hierarchy," which you will hear in most

tional device,"[82] allowing females to "externalize the cognitive problem [of deciding which male is worth reproducing with] to the [hierarchical] structure itself."[83] Dominance hierarchies, which are a more basic form of this, have been around for over 300 million years, dating back to at least lobsters.[84] It is a very old structure, which is significant in terms of what counts as our evolutionary environment.

The competence hierarchy is established by the pressures of sexual selection to sort out whose genes are "worthy" of replication, by valuing some character traits over others, and rewarding the attainment of those traits deemed "good" over the bad. This selective mechanism creates a multi-layered instability in our environment. Indeed, because we are not just reactive beings, and we see the

---

of his lectures and interviews. He means the same thing by these, but he no longer uses the word "dominance" (at least not consistently) because what he wants to indicate by these hierarchies is that you climb them with skill rather than with force.

[82] Jordan B. Peterson, "The Jordan B Peterson Podcast - Episode 4 - Religion, Myth, Science, Truth," Jordan Peterson, February 08, 2018, , accessed February 10, 2018, https://jordanbpeterson.com/podcasts/podcast-episode/episode-4/.

[83] TJBPP, #4..

[84] Peterson's fixation on lobsters is famously idiosyncratic, and this claim is everywhere in his work. It has to do with the fact that lobsters have the same neurochemical reward system as humans, utilizing serotonin.

world not only in terms of action but also potential futures,[85] group size is correlated to brain size. We must stand within multiple frames to act in and understand the world. What makes a man evolutionarily fit, as a result, is not merely physical strength, but, as we will see presently, moral strength.

The competence hierarchy is optimized for two functions: (1) scalability, it must be possible to make it to the top; and (2) status payoff, climbing the hierarchy improves social status and falling to the bottom diminishes it. Men, adapting to the hierarchy, have become better at climbing it, thereby improving the probability of leaving behind genetic material. One way men have done this is by paying attention to men who have risen to the top and by telling stories about them (sound familiar?). These men who scale the hierarchies are the heroes of our stories and myths. The competence hierarchy selects for heroes and breeds them: men imitate the heroes of myths, and this enables them to climb competence hierarchies.

That the hero has reached the top means he is admirable, and has noble principles, which introduces the possibility of reprehensible or disgraceful principles: those traits of the men at the bottom of the competence hierarchy (Daniel Dennett has briefly articulated a similar evolutionary grounding of our notions of right or wrong,[86] so this direction of

---

[85] See his second discussion with Sam Harris for further explication of this idea.

[86] See his comments on Robert Brandom's work: https://ase.tufts.edu/cogstud/dennett/papers/Brandom.pdf.

thought is not entirely foreign to Darwinism). From the traits of nobility and reprehensibility the ideas of good and evil are formed, and we can abstract from ten heroes a meta-hero: the saviors or enlightened ones of the major religious traditions across the world. Imitating the savior produces skills and traits that give one the greatest probability of climbing the set of all competence hierarchies.

If we take the metaphor of a game as an example, we can see this process more clearly. We all know a person who, when losing at a board game, will become frustrated. He might call others out for cheating when they are playing fair, he might quit before he can lose. At any rate, the beliefs he embodies while playing the game makes him insufferable. Rather than taking responsibility for his defeat, he blames it on the game or on the other players. He is the opposite of the hero. To imitate the hero would mean to transcend a victory or defeat in any given game by embodying beliefs that make one the kind of person that is invited to more games. We all have friends that are *good sports*, they are humble in victory or gracious in defeat.

To imitate the hero is to view life as larger than the demands of any given hierarchy. To live by the virtues of the greatest heroes we have in our myths is the key to this transcendence: to tell the truth, be courageous, and take responsibility for oneself. This is why Jordan Peterson believes we cannot get rid of myth: it distills not just information about sexual selection, but has developed to such a complexity that it grounds our conceptions of what it is to be good and, consequently, how to live a meaningful life.

The Great Convergence

The biological notion of competence hierarchies gives us an evolutionary explanation for the development of religion. According to this perspective, religion does not impinge, logically, on the world of the sciences. The fact that Christian fundamentalists are obsessed with a pseudo-scientific, quasi-theological doctrine of intelligent design is less indicative of an essential contradiction between science and religion and moreso of a confusion of discourses.[87] To separate them again, we can understand the functional significance of religious beliefs by looking to the meaning of these beliefs within religious contexts and, especially, religious myths. If we follow Peterson, and understand religion and science to operate according to different rules, we can see again, or perhaps for the first time, how they are mutually exclusive discourses, but in non-contradictory ways.

Peterson sets the religious symbols of myth within Darwinian evolution, thereby laying the groundwork for a unifying theory of science and religion. The main contribution of this theory is that it enables us to abstract the functional significance of religious myths and provides a way in which to understand how religion has given rise to the mod-

---

[87] D. Z. Phillips has made this point really well, indicating that as older discourses encounter newer discourses, the depth grammar of one can displace the depth grammar of the other.

ern world, without reducing religion to mere pre-scientific superstitious belief. To understand more specifically how we might understand religion functionally, we turn presently to Peterson's concept of God and then an explication of the good and meaningful life in his demythologization of religious symbols of myth.

4. THINKING CLEARLY ABOUT RELIGION: A PRELUDE TO PETERSON'S IDEAS ABOUT GOD AND FAITH

"This brings us to the greatest divide in the philosophy of religion, but one which is not always recognized. The greatest divide is not between those who give religious explanations and those who give secular explanations of the contingencies of human life for explanations in these contexts, and those who do not. The divide is between those who think it makes sense to look for explanations in these contexts, and those who do not."
Dewi Zephaniah Phillips, *Introducing Philosophy: The Challenge of Scepticism*[88]

Talk about the concept of God has become, once again, revivified in the wider culture. With the rise of Jordan Peterson to cultural and intellectual stardom, a rethinking of the meaning of religious beliefs and the role of religion in society is underway. Although, of course, there are many who remain entrenched in largely pre-scientific philosophical views regarding first mov-

_____

[88] Dewi Zephaniah Phillips, *Introducing Philosophy: The Challenge of Scepticism* (Oxford: Blackwell: 1997), 156.

ers or fundamentalist religious views concerning scriptural authorities, the most significant contribution Jordan Peterson has given to our cultural moment is the reintroduction of pragmatism to broader questions about religion, science, and philosophy. Pragmatism, seemingly dead after World War I, is now, once more, alive. To show the significance of this resurrection, I want to lay the groundwork for Jordan Peterson's ideas about faith and God by focusing solely on the question of the meaning of religious beliefs.

Religious beliefs have always fascinated me. They have been fertile ground for philosophical reflection, and dependable litmus tests for theories of knowledge. Before Jordan Peterson's entrance on the world stage, most popular talk surrounding religious beliefs either reduced them to claims about suprasensory objects, such as divine beings and supernatural powers, as we can see in the works of "New Atheists" like Sam Harris or Richard Dawkins; to subsets of larger political schemes, with writers like James Cone and Karl Marx; or to biological mechanisms that were mistaken by our ancestors to have sacred sources, as in Daniel Dennett's *Breaking the Spell*, where, in a *Westworld*-like fashion, we are told the predator-detector circuit probably made us believe in presences that were not there. As true and revelatory as all these accounts can be when applied to specific manifestations of religious belief and ritual (these all, to me, seem parasitic on making fundamentalism the essence of religious belief), they do not succeed in giving us a coherent conceptualization of what religious belief might be getting at as a whole.

Cautionary Notes: Thinking about Religion

I went skiing for the very first time two years ago in Colorado. My wife had skied before, but she was a bit insecure about her abilities this time around. After a few runs, we took a break to drink a hot beverage. She told me at this point that her last run she had succeeded in not falling once, and that, at junctures in which she might have failed at completing it successfully, she thought to herself, "You're okay. You know what you're doing. Just keep your feet parallel, stay calm, and use your hips to turn." This account became very interesting to me, because a few days later, we attended a Christmas Eve church service where the pastor's wife recounted a time when God "spoke" to her. She was driving home late one night at about two in the morning. She couldn't keep her eyes open, and she involuntarily rested them for a few moments. When she opened them, she was racing towards a semi, coming from the opposite direction. She said, at that point, she heard God tell her, "Don't put your hands on the steering wheel." She skidded along the side of the semi, coming to a stop on the side of the road, safely. She said that God was watching out for her, and she is thankful, still, for his love and grace.

From a general, descriptive level, these two stories are remarkably similar. Both involve situations in which inner-talk led to courses of actions which produced desirable outcomes. But they are conspicuously different in this way: whereas my wife, who does not talk of God in her everyday life, attributes her inner-voice to her conscience and reasoning, the pastor's wife thinks God told her what to do. The abyss between these accounts represents in a distilled, clear fashion, the state of inquiry concerning religious beliefs up to the present. Many people in our scientifically influenced culture would say the pastor's wife is just plainly wrong. If we replayed the scenario, there would be no divine being observably whispering in her ear. But this is precisely where we have gone too far. Have we understood the pastor's wife in the least?

What kind of account does religious belief require? We know that different situations can have different levels of analyses, some leading to more helpful and concrete conclusions than others. When my wife tells me, "I am mad at you for not doing the dishes," would a quantum mechanics account of the universe in that situation tell me what her anger means? Or what about if I knew the brain chemistry of anger, and could imagine in my head the brain states occurring when she told me she was angry, and understood the intricacies of speech processing and memory storage to such an extent that I could give an account of the sufficient physical conditions required for the sentence to be uttered in the first place? You might see my point: sometimes what is called an "explanation" is really just a different *description* of a phenomenon, rather than a true explanation, which would tell me not only the sufficient conditions of the phenomenon to exist but also *what it means for my behavior*. What does it mean that my wife is angry at me? Well it is partly that I can be a lazy, egocentric drone that ignores the perspectives and needs of others and refuse to participate in activities that cause me displeasure.

Now, what might we say in regards to religious belief? As the philosopher of religion D. Z. Phillips has pointed out,[89] disputes about religious beliefs usually treat them as if they are beliefs about facts. Talk about facts, however, just like talk about quantum mechanics, serves a different function than religious talk. For example, talk about facts happens when there is uncertainty, to rule out other possibilities. The essence of fact-talk is that its subject *might not have been*. We settle questions of fact by appealing to other facts. Applied to the example above, this does not account for the language of God. The pastor's wife had no question that it was God speaking to her. There is no question of doubt or other possibilities. Like Francis Collins, she could know all the facts a scientist like Richard Dawkins does, yet be certain of the reality of God. What can this mean?

She doesn't act like a person who believes in facts that don't exist: like a delusionary. She understands the principle of verification. The existence of God, for her, is not a fact; for to say that "Mom is in Indiana" is not like saying "God is in Heaven," although the sentences look the same. To say something is a fact is not to say anything about the thing itself, it is to indicate what it makes sense to say or do in relation to that thing. People who believe God exists are not like people who might believe uni-

---

[89] See the wonderful chapter, "Philosophy, Theology, and the Reality of God" from *Faith and Philosophical Inquiry*.

corns exist: they are not *factually mistaken*. The question of the reality of God is not like the question of whether an object exists, but like the question *what kind of reality* is the reality of "object?" To come to knowledge of a new fact is not tantamount to changing one's *understanding*, and this is precisely why the question of God is not a question about a fact of the universe. "Coming to see that there is a God involves seeing a new meaning in one's life, and being given a new understanding."[90] We can now begin to understand how the grammar of God is such that it does not make sense to say, on the one hand, that "God exists," while on the other, we are indifferent to God's existence.

Here, we can continue to follow Phillips: the meaning of religious beliefs is housed within the forms of life we call "religious." The criteria for the meaningfulness and veracity of religious beliefs are situated within the convergence of the logic of religious language and the actions of believers. Referring to our comments on pragmatism and the idea that our knowledge is embodied fundamentally, we are able to make the move situating religious belief, we can think, with Phillips, about the ways in which, "the child does not listen to the stories, observe religious practices, reflect on all this, and then form an idea of God out of the experience. The idea of God is being formed in the actual story-telling and religious services."[91] With James, we have to

---

[90] D. Z. Phillips, *Faith and Philosophical Enquiry* (Routledge & Kegan Paul Books: 1970), 18.

[91] Phillips, 5.

look to see what difference religious beliefs make in the world, while paying close attention to the language used to communicate this difference.

On the Grammar of "God is love"

To show how this might be done, I will briefly outline D. Z. Phillip's articulation of how the belief that "God is love" contains the essence of religious life.[92] After, we will look briefly at a few ways in which Jordan Peterson conceives of the concept of God to show how we might understand religious concepts *functionally*, that is to say, pragmatically. I want to caution at the outset that it is easy to misread the analysis here. If you begin with skepticism about the existence of God, and with the belief that what people talk about when they talk about God is a being like other beings, then you will miss the whole point of the analysis. Keeping in mind the example above, I want to give another example that might free us to think about religious language more broadly. Although these examples are not entirely commensurate, this should free up thinking to concerning the concept of God.

When we are children and are hurt, by bumping into the corner of a table for instance, or we trip and skin our knees on the ground, generally no words follow from these experiences, but maybe a loud yell, "OW!" and crying. As we age, and master more words, more classifications for experience and ourselves, and become cognizant of social expectations and self-image, the pain caused by bumping

---

[92] The outline is taken from his argument in *Phillips' Faith and Philosophical Enquiry*, 21- 33.

into the corner of a table or from skinning our knees no longer compels us to yell "OW!" or cry (at least, in general). We might whisper "OW," or if somebody is present we will say, "That hurt," or "That was painful." We might even get more specific and say, "That hurt. I skinned my knee on the sidewalk." There is a sense in which these latter, more nuanced and conceptually-heavy sentences that contain stories and descriptions are reducible to the child's, exasperated by pain, yell, "OW!" We say, "I just stubbed my foot on the table!" to indicate that we are in pain, to, in a way, sublimate the primal expression of irritation into a socially-acceptable package that invites others, in a way, to understand our pain without forcing them to participate in it (as others are "forced" to as one cries from pain).

In a similar way, we might compare the expression "God is love" with simpler expressions and experience. It is quite possible that "God is love," though it looks like "Camel is a mammal" does not function in the same way. Perhaps it is all reducible, in some situations, to a conviction, or a feeling, or a picture, or any number of things. Perhaps the sentence is just a stand in, and there are no real clear one-to-one references for each word. To go back to the pastor's wife, one can imagine her picturing, reimagining the near-miss, with the logic that the vehicles were somehow forced to move on their mutually exclusive routes. And, thinking of this, we might be able to see the consequences it would have for her life if she kept this picture at the front of her mind in every situation. This, in some way, is an intimation of how religious belief affects the lives of believers. This picture, for her, could be the meaning of "God is love."

But let us think about this conceptually, and about how the distinction between the eternal and the temporal ground this idea grammatically. D. Z. Phillips explains that the concept of the eternal is not, like skeptics claim, an epistemological category: it is not about an unverifiable point in time or a time after human history. It is rather a *kind of relation* toward others and the world, and it is illuminated in the notion of the "love of God."

To begin with, a primary way of thinking about human relationships in our secular society is through the concept of justice. With its logic, there is a distinction between *mine* and *yours*. To transgress against me is to take what is mine, and against you, I take what is yours. Extending the grammar of justice, we have notions of rights and responsibilities. Following the general notion today that everything is political, we can say that no relationship seems to escape the grammar of justice, not even erotic love, for even though "what's mine is yours" becomes transformed into an *ours*, what is *ours* is now functionally equivalent to *mine* in its distinction from *theirs*.

Similarly, just as justice is contingent on the attainment of certain conditions in the world, so too is erotic love: it depends on the wellbeing and existence of the beloved. Oftentimes, the death of a significant other can be such a blow that it rids life of its meaning. It is true that, say, as love fades, the beloved is replaced with another, thereby displacing the original relationship. But it still remains the case that the equation for erotic love is $1 + 1$ and consequently requires that certain conditions in the world be fulfilled: "it depends on how things go, it may change, and it may end in failure."[93]

On the other hand, Christianity intends to speak of a different kind of relationship, an unconditional kind of love, a love of *neighbor*. "What is more, it claims that this love is internally related to the love of God; that is, that without knowing what this love is, one cannot know what the love of God is either."[94] "The neighbour is not loved because of his being a parent, lover, or friend, but simply because of his being."[95] To achieve this kind of love requires, as the Bible states, a dying to oneself. We are here contrasting the language of justice with the language of eternity.

"Much of what is meant by seeing things from the point of view of the eternal can be grasped by understanding what it means to die to the expectations created by desire or moral rights."[96]

Many religious teachers speak of the necessity of 'dying to oneself'. Often they are referring to the refusal to use one's power when one is the stronger member of an unequal relationship. When the inequality is marked as in slavery, the

---

[93] Phillips, 23.

[94] Phillips, 22.

[95] Phillips, 24.

[96] Phillips, 51.

weaker member is in danger of ceasing to be a person. In order to renounce one's power one must not fix one's attention on *how* people are: useful or useless for one, desirable or undesirable, morally deserving or undeserving, but on the fact *that* they are.[97]

The notion of dying to oneself functions to enact a change of perspective, specifically to change one's perspective from a basic, narcissistic self-preservationism that looks out into the world of people and objects to see whom or what can be used for one's purposes.

A recent experience of mine illustrated this move clearly to me. I grew up with two sisters and a brother in a single-mother home until I was a teenager. My mother is a manic depressive hypochondriac. She hardly ever left her bedroom in my teenager years. Though only 16 years older than me, her mental and physical health (which has since been declining after becoming addicted to opiates) is probably that of a person twice to three times her chronological age. When I was around 13, she married my stepfather, after meeting him at a party. He was always a very nice, hardworking man, despite having muscular dystrophy and diabetes, and, although I can hardly say he was treated with respect much of the time, he loved and cared for us as if we were his own children and never complained about the burdens life had handed to him. He was a genuinely happy man who enjoyed being alive.

---

[97] Phillips, 51.

While I was working on this book, he passed away. It happened out of the blue. I had not spoken with him for about a year, and it had been longer since I last visited with him. My mother left him soon after I graduated high school, and my avoidance of her, for the sake of getting myself together, led to my unfortunate avoidance of him. On many occasions I promised I would visit him, but I never did. He had always been very kind to me, but I had become obsessed with productivity, building a self-image that didn't include my mother's voice, and my own plans. I just never made the time to see him. At his funeral, his brother had told me he talked about me a lot and always spoke highly of me.

I grew up in a small, poor town of about 2,000 people in northern Indiana. Many of my friends and acquaintances are conservative, evangelical Christians. So I think about religious belief quite a bit. As I was working through some of the issues of guilt and grief that followed my stepfather's death, I realized how much easier it would be if I believed in the afterlife. I would think eventually I could be forgiven, that I could perhaps say a few words that my stepfather could hear from wherever he is, and that I would see him again someday and could make known how much he meant to me and how sorry I am for effectively cutting him out of my life. I was, at least, always happy to know he was alive somewhere and I knew deeply that despite his circumstances he had a joy nothing could take away from him.

Thinking about the belief in the afterlife, I asked myself what would change about my behavior if, for the sake of thought, I did believe in it and the existence of God. This happened to have been my most significant question. One thing that came to mind was that I would accept that we never have enough time with the ones we love: whether we are on good terms or bad, people are taken away from us without closure. It is, as they say, "God's plan." Another thing that occurred to me is that I would act as if I could somehow be ultimately forgiven for my sins of omission and commission against my stepfather, and that meant that I could be free to act in such a way that if my stepfather were alive I would behave as if I could make amends. Effectively this meant that I had to rethink how I was living and reprioritize my life: to no longer see things from the perspective of my everyday routines, interests, and plans. I would rather prioritize the people who, out of some miracle, choose to relate to me, and prioritize them for no other reason than that they are in my life. The fact that we exist at all, and come together in moments of vulnerability, love, and care is a complete wonder that just astounds me.

D. Z. Phillips, again, encapsulates this move of the religious succinctly:

> the attitude of the deeply religious man is not determined by looking at things from the midst of them. To say that his attitude is other than this is what is meant by saying that his attitude is other than the world's way of regarding things. His view is of the world as a whole, and

determines the nature of the world for him. Hs world is a different world from that of the man who sees objects from the midst of them. *How* the world is is the same for both of them, but what they make of the world is different.[98]

This, Phillips believes, is the key to understanding religious language, especially talk about God. The fact that the perspective changes from the self to existence itself means that life cannot be robbed of its meaning despite failures, tragedies, and even death.

What he [the believer] is asked to do is not to love the loved one in such a way that the love of God becomes impossible. The death of the beloved must not rob life of its meaning, since for the believer the meaning of life is found in God. The believer claims that there is a love that will not let one go whatever happens. This is the love of God, the independence of which from what happens is closely bound up with the point of calling it eternal.[99]

Indeed, he continues,

Love of God is not the only form of religious belief, but I believe it is the primary form. That is a *grammatical* observation. We could not have anything we know as Christianity if other

---

[98] Phillips, 54-55.

[99] Phillips, 23.

forms of belief were to become the rule....Love of God is logically prior to other forms of belief.[100]

To pull this all together, think about the differences between "Mom is in Indiana" and "God is in Heaven." On the surface, we can say it appears that these two sentences are indicating the same things but about different beings and places. How we interpret the logic of sentences by looking at their surface logic is called *surface grammar*. The surface grammar of religious statements in many situations seems like the depth grammar of scientific statements. The depth grammar of a sentence is the logic of the sentence given by its speaker. The logic of a scientific sentence, then, assumes the framework of natural laws, the separation of affect from objects, and the like. What D. Z. Phillips is pointing out is that the depth grammar of religious statements assumes a view of the world as a whole, which is to say a view of the world which does not depend on how things go. The functional consequence of this is that life cannot be robbed of its meaning by how things go, and it allows us to adapt to tragedy without destroying us. This is all we can say in this brief work, but below we will see, further, and in a different way, how religious belief can be interpreted functionally.

---

[100] Phillips, 68.

Peterson and a Functional Account of God

"We're in these hierarchies, many of them across centuries. We're trying to figure out what the guiding principle is. We're trying to extract out the core of the guiding principles, and we turn that into a representation of a pattern of being. That's God. It's an abstracted ideal, and it manifests itself in personified form. That's ok, because what we're trying to get at is, in some sense, the essence of what it means to be a properly functioning, properly social, and properly competent individual."[101]

"Whatever it is that is you has this capacity to experience reality and to transform it, which is a very strange thing. You can conceptualize the future in your imagination, and then you can work and make that manifest—participate in the process of creation. That's one way of thinking about it. That's why I think Genesis 1 relates the idea that human beings are made in the image of the divine."[102]

To move from D. Z. Phillips to Jordan Peterson is relatively simple: with less emphasis on the language, we turn to the behavioral significance belief in God has for believers as the predominate phenomena to be interpreted. As we have noted, one of Peterson's fundamental claims is that beliefs are

---

[101] Jordan B. Peterson, "Biblical Series I: Introduction to the Idea of God Transcript," Jordan Peterson, June 02, 2018, accessed June 03, 2018,
https://jordanbpeterson.com/transcripts/biblical-series-i/.

[102] Peterson, BSI.

embodied before they are abstracted into language and codified in doctrines. The claim is consistent with our notion above that the sentence "God is love" can have different meanings for different people, and in some cases it may simply be an expression of a conviction, much like "I have a pain in my knee" is reducible to the expression "OW!"; or it might be indicative of a disposition toward life as a whole, as Phillips discussed. That these beliefs are embodied first means that at times we have no reasons for these beliefs, or that we can be wrong about the expression of our beliefs. Indeed, "The ritual lasts long after the reasons have been forgotten."[103] This can account for the many confusions of discourses between science and religion that occur today, especially in the Intelligent Design movement. Similarly, sometimes, the language of the beliefs can last long after the embodied significance is outlived, such as when the language of the divine becomes colloquial, as in "God damnit," or when, under distress, a person might yell, "Oh my God!"

Without comparing the beliefs of the religious with the claims of scientists, we can begin to situate religious expressions within the realm of strictly *human* existence, rather than objective descriptions of human existence. If we think again about the example of the angry wife, knowing quantum theory will not help me *understand* why she is angry at me, or even what her anger means. The same is true when scientific conceptions of the universe are imposed on religious expressions: although "Mom is in Indiana" and "God is in Heaven" appear similar

---

[103] Peterson, BSI.

on the surface, they lead to dramatically different consequences for behavior.

These notes are all simply landmarks on our map of the phenomena of the religious. It is always possible, and in our time too easily accepted without second thought, to reduce religious expressions, rituals, and experiences to one-dimensional, easily disregarded phenomena. It is Peterson's contention that this is a mistake, as they appear infinitely deep. Instead of following the move of reduction, Peterson has usefully provided many functional definitions of faith, the concept of God, and many other ideas associated with Christianity, such as the resurrection. Here we just want to look at a few, to understand the framework from which he is working.

I want to begin by pointing out that Jordan Peterson, when speaking about the Bible, is not doing theology. He is, rather, giving a *psychological* interpretation of a religious text. What this means is first of all he leaves questions about whether religious beliefs are true in a scientific sense off the table. He is not interested in apologetics. Nor is he interested in developing doctrines that might one day support the growth of a new Protestant denomination. In the biblical lectures series, Peterson is attempting to delineate the psychological utility of religious beliefs and expressions. As he says, the Bible is not interested in scientific truth, but truth on the level of Shakespeare: "truths to live by."[104] The Bible is made of *stories*.

---

[104] Peterson, BSI.

And so if you know that what the Bible stories, and stories in general, are trying to represent is the structure of the lived experience of conscious individuals, you open up the possibility of a whole different realm of understanding. It eliminates the contradiction that's been painful for people, between the objective world and the claims of religious stories.[105]

Indeed, just as good literature is attentive to human conflict and psychology, the Bible is as well. Peterson's argument seems to be that if there are problems of action and life common to us all, then there might also be patterns of being adoptable by anyone that would at least put us in positions where these problems do not destroy us. The philosopher Ludwig Wittgenstein said something similar in reference to religious ceremonies. It is curious, after all, that, if religious beliefs had nothing to do with what is real, there would not be an infinite plurality of them. That they deal with real issues of life seems self-evident, according to Wittgenstein: "If I wanted to make up a festival, it would die out very quickly or be modified in such a manner that it corresponds to a general inclination of the people."[106]

So what is the conflict common to us all? Jordan Peterson thinks it is about the fact that we know we will someday die, that someday all of our ac-

---

[105] Peterson, BSI.

[106] Ludwig Wittgenstein, *Philosophical Occasions: 1912-1951*, ed. James Carl Klagge (Indianapolis: Hackett, 1994), 147.

complishments, relationships, and passions will come to nothing.

> Can we have the being that requires limitation and suffering and also simultaneously transcend that by our mode of being? I believe that the Biblical stories are one of the human imagination's best attempts to address and answer that question. That's what the entire story is about. The first of it is the catastrophe of the collapse of self-consciousness, and the entrance of humanity into history. The rest of it is, ok, now we're in history; now we know that we're going to die, we know about our mortality, and we're conscious of our own being. Is there a mode of acting in the world that allows that to be justifiable? Or, maybe even more, that allows that to be triumphant?[107]

This is the question of the human condition: Is there a mode of acting that allows life to be bearable, despite its inevitable end? This is the question we will explore more fully next chapter, but for now it is enough to ask the question. It colors every interpretation Peterson has about the Bible. Consequently, the dominant theme Peterson sees playing out in the text is that the hero accepts mortality, with all the betrayals, injustices, tragedies, and pain, and, despite that, lives courageously, as if existence itself were fundamentally good. "Ok, so the question is, what are the principles that guide our behav-

---

[107] Peterson, BSI.

iour? Well, that's something like what the archaic Israelites meant by 'God.'"[108] What are these principles? Peterson sees these housed in the trinitarian conception of God.

We recognize that there is an interpretative structure that has been handed down to us by tradition, through language and rituals, that allows us to confront reality courageously. This is the idea of God the Father: we acquire a depth of experience by having the tools and support of tradition behind us. Tradition tells us already what we will fail at because we are historical creatures. We have built-in conceptions of our weaknesses and failures, and it gives us a way of forgiving ourselves, by telling us that we cannot but fall short. Importantly, it also gives us a way of transcending these. This is the meaning of the rites and rituals. Like it is written in the Psalms: "Your word is a lamp to my feet and a light to my path."[109] God the Father, for Peterson, also encompasses the notion of the future: that we can bargain with our fates by acting *properly*.

Continuing, the concept of the Son represents the one who embodies the tradition and works out its principles in every new situation. Because he embodies the tradition, he accepts the burdens of being which tradition has already outlined for him. Tradition tells him that death is a constant companion, that betrayals, unstoppable decay, and moral trials are essential aspects of life. But tradition also tells him of the good, of the communion with the superordinate principle, and of the kind of existence

---

[108] Peterson, BSI.
[109] NRSV, Psalm 119:105

possible if you stay in line, tell the truth, and live courageously, in "the idea of Christ's voluntary sacrifice of his own life. His presupposition was something like, I'm going to act as if God is good, and I'm going to play that out right to the end. That becomes something like a divine pattern."[110] The Son accepts the tragedies of life as if he were in part responsible for them, and then, like God, creates novel order out of chaos, declaring what he creates through speech and action, "Good."

Lastly, the Spirit, for Peterson, is, in part, the vision of the self that lives a life that justifies suffering. It is something like conscience, and the human soul, that, if we always did what we *ought* to do, we would be baptized by it, in some sense, just like the Son. In reference to competence hierarchies, Peterson thinks the concept of the Holy Spirit is a picture of transcending all hierarchies, to be able to participate in the sum total of all hierarchies without being bound to any: it knows the rules, the virtues, which allow success in all of them, and, thereby, understands the divine pattern of being that allows one to live meaningfully despite suffering:

You imagine an infinite plane, and in the infinite plane there's nothing but pyramids. Inside the pyramids there are strata of people, everywhere, as far as you can look. Some of the pyramids are tall, and some of them are short; they

---

[110] Jordan B. Peterson, "Biblical Series II: Genesis 1: Chaos & Order Transcript," Jordan Peterson, April 17, 2018, accessed June 10, 2018, https://jordanbpeterson.com/transcripts/biblical-series-ii/.

overlap. The plane is endless, and those are all the positions to which you could rise. Everybody's inside the pyramids, sort of camped up, trying to move toward the top. And then there's the possibility of sailing across, overtop all of them, and seeing how the structure itself works. That's the eye that floats above the pyramid, and it sees the structure itself. The highest order of being is not to be at the top of the pyramid: it's to use the discipline you attain by striving towards the top of the pyramid to release yourself from the pyramid and move one step up. I think that's one of the things instantiated in the idea, for example, of the Holy Ghost.[111]

Looking Ahead: From God to Faith

If we follow Peterson's lead, then we can see that religion is not merely a pre-scientific enterprise, based fundamentally on error-ridden theories of the cause and effect continuum of nature. As Wittgenstein sarcastically remarked regarding *The Golden Bough*:

Frazer says that it is very hard to discover the error in magic—and that is why it has lasted so long—because, for example, an incantation that is supposed to bring rain certainly seems efficacious sooner or later. But then it is surely remarkable that people don't realize earlier that sooner or later it's going to rain anyhow.[112]

---

[111] Peterson, BSII.

[112] Wittgenstein, 121.

Against the background of the reductions of religion to mere superstition, Peterson has given the secular world new ways in which to take religious belief seriously, new avenues to study myth as part of the history of cultural evolution. He has done this by giving us functional definitions of concepts that, for many, seem empty at best and a naive, wish fulfillment desires at worst. Now that we have briefly examined his concept of God and how it connects with the central problems of death and suffering in human experience, we can turn to faith, and its functional import for the solution to this problem. As we will see, the concept of life as a whole, of telling the truth, and Peterson's understanding of the logos, though interpreted psychologically, are not in fact foreign to Christian theology. They find their places at home within it. Yet, what Peterson has done is not give us a new theology, but a way to understand theology without being captive to its language, Christianity's institutional history, and the socio-political baggage Christianity is associated with in the West.

5. THE LIFE THAT JUSTIFIES SUFFERING

"There is something irreducible about suffering."
Jordan Peterson, on the *Joe Rogan Experience*[113]

"That which you most need will be found where you least want to look."
Jordan Peterson, on *Under the Skin*[114]

Many detractors criticize Peterson's interpretations of religion. They claim he uses the ideas of religion to support beliefs he already held; that they are, at base, idiosyncratic. But anyone who has read major thinkers who have shaped the West—like William James, Friedrich Nietzsche, Alfred Whitehead, and Ludwig Wittgenstein; the psychologists C. G. Jung, Robert Kegan, and Carl Rogers; the theologians Rudolf Bultmann, Paul Tillich, and Friedrich Schleiermacher—would know this is at best a rather shallow conclusion. There are a multitude of interpreters who came before Peterson who both analyzed religion with similar methods and reached analogous conclusions. This is not to take anything away from him, for I

---

[113] JRE, #958.

[114] UTS,# 46.

think his particular integration of psychology, religious ideas, and evolutionary theory is novel and exactly what is needed in this cultural moment to begin a serious re-examination of the place of religion in secular society. Yet, I also want to encourage readers to pick up the works of the other authors mentioned here to continue the discussion Peterson has so brilliantly prompted today.

Theology after Wilhelm Herrmann

To support my claim, I want to briefly suggest a modern precursor to Peterson who has, to a large extent, remained in the shadows: Wilhelm Herrmann, the teacher of two major theological giants of the twentieth century, Rudolf Bultmann and Karl Barth. Again, in what follows, we will not consider the basic element of religion to be something like "belief in a higher power," if "belief" is defined as "the acceptance of a list of propositions as true without any warrant." The mediation of the world that occurs in religion is not the same kind of mediation that occurs in the sciences, as has already been suggested. Rather than dividing up the world into objects and taxonomizing their traits, religion works within the world of valence, or the functional significance of things. Furthermore, we can also understand religious belief as *orienting* actions toward reality as a whole. With Wilhelm Herrmann we begin to appreciate this:

> ...the essential content of religion does not consist in any kind of ideas of transcendent things; its essence is rather a particular way in which

man experiences the whole of reality; he possesses religion when this reality, which first of all appears to all men as an indefinite plurality, becomes for him an ordered whole or universe. This happens when a man perceives in reality the unity of an inexhaustible life. . . . (Thus) he is the religious man who, in every experience which moves his spirits, hears a single, living Power speak to his soul.[115]

As Willard Reed goes on to explicate in *Against the Science of Delusion*, the experience of the religious person is an experience of the unification of reality, which, in one way, creates the inner life of the self for the first time, and, in another, calls one to respond to reality as a whole, as a person who is both an essential part of this reality and yet dependent on it. This does not mean that faith is some kind of observable event, however, or that the beliefs of the faithful function to justify faith itself. It is rather that the life of the believer is the confirmation to the believer. Reed translates Herrmann to explain this view: "life creates its own justification through its act."[116] Continuing later, Reed writes, "The truth of faith shows itself in the truth of a life of one's own."

---

[115] Herrmann, *Systematic Theology*, p. 32f. Emphasis added. Taken from Willard K. Reed Jr., "Against the science of delusion: Doing theology in the legacy of Wilhelm Herrmann," (PhD Diss., Claremont Graduate School, 1993), 95.

[116] Herrmann, "Neu gestellte Aufgaben der evangelischen Theologie," p. 261. Taken from Reed, 99.

The very idea of "the truth of faith" will be offensive to some. If truth is not understood as correspondence to reality, how else might it be meaningfully used? Yet, one can understand what is meant in this statement and still retain this notion of truth. Faith is self-validating in that its structuring of the self creates the lens by which the self understands itself. Though this may seem circular, it is more complex than that. For some interpreters of religion, the structure of faith *is* the authentic structure of the self. We cannot understand the world, for instance, until we can separate ourselves from it. In unifying the world and unifying the self, the two are separated in the same movement by becoming parts of a whole. For them, the origins of the self, and the origins of truth, dwell in the experience of faith. Reed writes, "The self-revelation of God which is self-authentication is experienced as the revelation of the true self of the individual person."[117] For Reed and Herrmann, as for Jung, God is a symbol of individuation. The power of faith comes not in its rational explanation of the universe, but in its functional significance: the creation of the self as response-able to the world as a whole.

Although briefly, we have seen that Herrmann understood faith to inspire an orientation toward reality as a whole, involve the creation of the self, and impose the burden of responsibility. He has one more thing in common with Peterson: he believes the origins of religion rest on *truthfulness*. As Reed writes:

---

[117] Reed, 107.

Christian faith, for Herrmann, pertains to the *Wirklichkeit* known to moral experience, i.e., the experience of the individual. The realm of the ethical, the individual, is the arena of religion. In this context *Wirklichkeit* does not refer to the "unending multiplicity of things and experiences in space and time," but rather to "the specifically human mode of experience." This "human mode of experience" is, according to Herrmann, a quest of "moral seriousness" for an answer to the question concerning the meaning of one's existence. This is the desire for truthfulness [Wahrhaftigkeit] in our own inner life. The reality of inner life shows itself not as the scientifically verifiable reality of science, but in the reality of one's encounter with a transcendent power which brings one to true individuality, to true personhood.[118]

Wilhelm Herrmann's work on the origin or religion and the meaning of faith is a significant precursor to Peterson's own ideas, at least chronologically, if he is not an influence for Peterson personally. Especially in regards to Peterson's connection of truth to the meaningful life, Herrmann has a compelling argument for this connection and provides an earlier articulation of the idea: "The way to religion lies for each person in the desire for the truthfulness (Wahrhaftigkeit) of his own inner life." "The way to religion lies in the willingness to bring truth (Wahrheit) and clarity into our experience." "I see the way to religion in the question concerning

---

[118] Reed, 61-62.

the truthfulness (Wahrhaftigkeit) of the individual life, and the origin of religion in the creation of a true (wahrhaftig) life, for which neither the decision of my own will nor any science can be of help to me."[119] Peterson, we see, is not without his peers, finding one in a profoundly seminal figure in modern theology.

The Two Fundamental Categories of the Unconscious

To return to the task at hand, now that a brief Darwinian account of religion has been given in the previous chapter, and the map to a functionalist explanation of religious belief suggested, we can proceed to a fuller exposition of religious belief and forms of life. With this in mind, we move to what Peterson considers the two fundamental concepts that form the logic of religious language: order and chaos. These are functionally two ways of apprehending reality *as a whole*. Later, we will see how it is not that the religious person works to reside in order, or acts to avoid chaos, but that a combination of the two sets the stage for responsibility and personhood. Concluding, we will also see how speech, and telling the truth, are central to this endeavor.

The world is best primarily conceptualized as a forum for action, where the basic categories of thought divide the things of reality into obstacles or

---

[119] Reed, 68. For a brilliant analysis of this idea, see *Against The Science of Delusion: Doing Theology In The Legacy Of Wilhelm Herrmann* by Willard Reed, especially chapter 2 section 3 entitled "The Way to Religion."

tools, predators or kin:[120] when we encounter strangers, our predator circuitry processes their appearance, and when we hear familiar words or see friends and family, a completely different physiological process frames the world and our situation in it.[121] The seemingly distinct categories of tools and obstacles and kin and predators collapse into two more fundamental categories that delineate our basic situation in the world. The fight, flight, or freeze response, abstracted, situates us in the category of *chaos*, where nothing is predictable, controllable, or known, and we discover obstacles; whereas the world of order and family, where our intentions cause expected consequences, and tools function as assumed, brings us to the category of *order*. Chaos and order phenomenologically structure our worlds (this, perhaps, was first discovered by Mircea Eliade in *The Sacred and the Profane*).

Chaos is not the place you want to be, and it is no surprise that this forms the basis for the mythological conception of the underworld. It is where you are when all the skills you've learned, where everything you believed to be good and true, and where all that has worked well in the past, no longer

---

[120] In his debate with Matt Dillahunty, Peterson takes the philosophically pragmatic position that it is extremely difficult to tell the difference between what is real and what is useful. And, indeed, according to his conception of the world as a forum for action, this claim seems to follow.

[121] JRE, #958. Peterson repeats this claim and similar ones, with different examples, in nearly every presentation I've heard. For an extensive, academic treatment, see *Maps of Meaning*.

works or make sense of where you find yourself. In chaos, your brain stops thinking about the future, initiates emergency preparation mode, shifts cortisol levels, activates left and right cortices, disinhibits limbic and motivational systems, and causes you to sweat and lose sleep.[122] You literally pay a price for being in chaos: your body, going into superhuman mode, self-destructs the longer it is in chaos. You are in the unknown, and your body is preparing for anything: for fight, flight, or to freeze. Chaos is the underworld of mythology: the dragon's lair, or the belly of the whale.

Chaos, though a structure of thought, is best conceived of as a *place*; for, again, we are talking about the perception of the functional significance of things, and our beliefs are embodied before they are abstracted. Chaos structures our perception, thereby sketching the things in the world. Peterson has a great example of this: imagine you're married for ten years. You work hard to support your family, you do all the right things, at least all the things expected of a *good* spouse. When you come home from work one day, your significant other reveals he or she has been involved in an affair spanning the last couple of years. You're not just confused or shocked when you hear this. You're in *hell*. Just minutes ago, your world was exactly what you expected it to be. You had finished the routine of

---

[122] Jordan B. Peterson, "The Jordan B Peterson Podcast - Episode 1 - Reality & The Sacred," Jordan Peterson, February 08, 2018, accessed February 17, 2018, https://jordanbpeterson.com/podcasts/podcast-episode/episode-1/.

work. You were coming home to spend the rest of the day with your spouse, perhaps go out on a date at a restaurant, talk about your days, and the like. Now what will you do? The person you have been married to for a decade now appears like a stranger. You didn't know him or her, but you thought you did. Your marriage has been deteriorating in front of you, but you thought it was going well. And that means fundamental beliefs you had about yourself are likely wrong. Who are you, that you could be deceived in such a fundamental way? You have to re-examine everything. The fundamental beliefs you had in the past will not serve your life in the future. What does the house you're standing in now *mean*? What about your job? The future is lightless, with no indication as to what will come next. This is what chaos looks like.

Order, on the other hand, is the place you are when everything works exactly as you expect, within the ordering of the competence hierarchy, and in turn your beliefs about what is true and good provide sufficient aims for action. Consequently, people will protect their competence hierarchies, even as they don't benefit, because it is better to be a slave and know what is going on than it is to be thrown naked into the jungle in the middle of the night.[123] Imagine if the same scenario above played out except without infidelity the day continued ex-

---

[123] Jordan B. Peterson, "Jordan Peterson: Dragons, Divine Parents, Heroes and Adversaries: A Complete Cosmology of Being," YouTube, June 16, 2014, accessed August 20, 2016, https://www.youtube.com/watch?v=nqONu6wDYaE.

actly as expected. That is order. And it is no wonder people desire to protect it. But, taken alone, neither chaos nor order is completely habitable if one also wants to take responsibility for themselves and live a meaningful life. "Chaos is where things are so complex that you can't handle it, and order is where things are so rigid that it's too restrictive."[124] We will return to this shortly.

These fundamental forms of perception set the stage for our bodily, intuitive understanding of the world (which Peterson believes is primary to all thought); our brains are adapted to these meta-realities—hierarchies and archetypes—as opposed to the realities of objects and things. What sets our environment, at any given time, is not necessarily the objects or beings that surround us, but whether we are positioned in chaos or order. Indeed, these two categories constitute what Peterson means by "reality."

The Conflict Inherent in Existence and the Problem of Evil

The meta-realities of chaos and order introduce an irresolvable tension at the center of human experience. Chaos is, of course, a terrible place to be, for we do not know who we are when we are in chaos. But order is not completely safe either. By simplifying the complexity of the world, order can render us vulnerable to the shock of novelty. What enables us to thrive in the present might not prepare us for flourishing in the future, it might actually prevent it.

---

[124] Peterson, "Dragons, Divine Parents."

Yet, the future which is unbearable to the present always appears as chaos. We, therefore, must move into chaos to continue to survive: to stand between chaos and order and make a new order. This constant back and forth between order and chaos is the bedrock of the problem of evil: is existence worth the suffering? Peterson, here, distinguishes between *tragedies*, like natural disasters, and *suffering*, caused both by our disposition toward the world as a whole and the reality of malevolence (the fact that sometimes people pursue the suffering of others for the sake of suffering). Responses to tragedy are not necessitated by the tragic events themselves, despair is not compulsory, for sometimes we face tragedies heroically. Because of this, tragedies are not included under the problem of evil for Peterson. The true problem of evil, for him, is the problem of suffering.

The problem of suffering manifests itself in different forms in order and chaos: these forms are the archetypes. When order causes suffering, it is represented symbolically in myth as the tyrant father. Sometimes what is true today isn't true enough to serve life: to allow for genuine human flourishing as the potentialities of the future are actualized, changing the present. When this is the case, the realm of order, if it is forced upon us as the *only* way to proceed, as transcendental constraints on action and belief, is tyrannical. The tyrannical fathers of myth are the kings who force tradition upon the heroes, by the demand that they act only by the codes of conduct derived from the past, making the heroes unable to face the threats of the future. The heroes, in turn, are those who do not obey, but, somehow still grounded in tradition, encounter the chaos with novel conduct.

Another problem with order is it tends to simplify the world into shallow categories that don't adequately account for the reality that confronts us. The evil figure in myth, the one who is hyperrational, like Lucifer, who falls in love with his own creations and excludes the possibility of the transcendent, which is uncontrollable and inconceivable, embodies this archetype of order. Here, Peterson places the origins of ideology. The very idea of the transcendent is operative in our everyday lives when we act in the world as if it is full of potentials rather than final realities; and when these realities are reduced and simplified into basic, unchanging objects like doctrines or codes of conduct, the possibility of change, and therefore growth, development, and progress, is excluded at the outset. This is how the transcendent is removed by order. Opposed to this, a correct conception of order, is more like the Garden of Eden: no matter how perfectly society is set up, there will be something you don't want that appears—the serpent. As an agent of chaos, the serpent essentially undermines lasting stability. Order can become chaos in an instant. A healthy relationship with order involved placing one foot in order, the other in chaos.

But, the problems of chaos are equally destabilizing and debilitating. The archetypal shadow side of chaos is the devouring mother: confronted by the potentialities of the future, or the deep unknown of the present, some people are crushed by despair.

People who find themselves in chaos, if they have gotten there by choosing what is expedient over what is worthwhile, by lying to themselves and projecting their inadequacies onto the world and others rather than being honest with themselves and paying attention to how their beliefs might not account for reality or how their actions might be making things worse, will despair in times of suffering.[125] The positive side of chaos is symbolically represented as mother nature: the great creator, the origin of possibility. When confronted honestly, chaos can bring a new order, where a novel flourishing is possible.

We are inclined to cling to order, or close our eyes in chaos: we all know of men who never grew up, who have the emotional intelligence of a twelve-year-old but the musculature of a brute in its prime. Clinging to order makes us resentful, for who we thought we were, and the values that grounded our perception of reality, no longer provide anything to orient ourselves with. Like Moses, we do all the "right" things but never reach the promised land: the land of achieved aims. In this state, it remains convenient for people to divide the world into the righteous and the damned so that whatever resentment and bitterness and hatred is in

---

[125] Of course, there are older conceptions of evil than what Christianity presents; however, Peterson thinks Christianity has the most robust conception of evil because it combines older conceptions with the idea that the solution to evil is to confront it, as an individual, and choose against it: to not simply recognize its objective reality in events or groups or others, but its subjective reality within the self, and then to choose whatever leads us away from suffering and evil.

their hearts can be ignored, and so too can a blind eye be turned to every way in which they participate in the problem they are trying to overcome.

Those who cling to order are devoured by chaos. This is a bottomless abyss, for the devouring mother finds you in despair. The archetype of the devouring mother brings a terminal screen over the eyes of the possessed, motivating actions by the belief that "It is better if it never existed at all." People who act out this belief make suffering worse: despair ignites the flames of revenge, the desire to strike back at being for the crime of existence, to turn against being all around us and seek complete destruction. In this state, when we suffer, we delight in the suffering of others; the origin of suffering is the awareness of our own vulnerabilities, where malevolence is the intentional exploitation of the vulnerabilities of others. "Evil is the production of suffering for its own sake."[126] Chaos is an ocean of darkness, and the deeper we descend, the more primal the monsters we discover.

Here we find the connection between the snake, Lucifer, and the concept of evil. Mythology has figured out, especially in Christianity, that the worst snake isn't a real snake, but rather the internal "snake" of malevolence: the snake inside a person. And this, Peterson thinks, partially explains the origin of our idea of evil. First the snake was external, moving somewhere in the environment; then the snake was believed to dwell inside a person.

---

[126] Jordan B. Peterson, "Jordan Peterson: What Matters," YouTube, March 30, 2013, accessed August 05, 2016, https://www.youtube.com/watch?v=A5216ZJVbVs.

Then the snake inside person A and B became identical, which is the idea of Lucifer, the "snake" that possesses person A and B. Finally the concept of evil—the abstract pattern of being characterized by the snake, Lucifer, that lives inside everyone. There is a way of living that confronts Lucifer head-on, demanding the keys to Hell, so that we may overcome it, and reach Heaven.

When in chaos, Peterson calls us to pay attention, because sometimes the things that we most value are what got us to Hell in the first place. The world is systematized and viewed by reference to our values, so it makes sense that when we are in chaos, and we do not understand where we are, our deepest values may be the cause of our descent. Under these circumstances, to sacrifice the thing most valuable to us, as a religious principle, is the idea that a complete conversion is sometimes what it takes to live well. In this way, life demands the best from us, which sometimes means sacrificing who we are for who we may become.[127] Is nothing better than something: would it have been better had being never existed at all? The God of myth says no, which is another way of saying our myths have answered this question of suffering for us, articulating the kind of life that overcomes suffering. This is the meta-hero archetype, or the notion of the sav-

---

[127] Jordan B. Peterson, "The Jordan B Peterson Podcast - Episode 13 - Maps of Meaning 10 - 13," Jordan Peterson, February 08, 2018, accessed February 22, 2018, https://jordanbpeterson.com/podcasts/podcast-episode/episode-13/.

ior.[128] Between the wise king and mother nature, the hero stands; which is to say that the mediating force between chaos and order is consciousness. The battle between good and evil isn't between states or between individuals but it is an internal and moral battle: between malevolence and benevolence.

The idea of the sacred itself is functionally, for Peterson, about the essential nature of existence. What we believe about the divine throughout the centuries has been a projection of what we take the meaning of existence to be. One of the conclusions of Christianity is that if we act towards the divine as if it is nothing but good, then it is more likely to be true in the world. This takes both courage and faith: courage because it is not self-evident that suffering is ever overcome, that we will ever ascend from Hell to Heaven, that chaos will ever end; and faith because it is possible that suffering may never, indeed, be overcome. But the idea of faith is that you make the case that being *is* good by acting that way, and, to truly have faith, to act as if being is good and play that out until the end. This is an interesting solution to the problem of suffering. If we act toward existence as if it is good, then we will be willing to *sacrifice* for it. We will be more susceptible to seek out the origins of the problems of existence in ourselves, thereby exhibiting adaptive patterns of behavior and thinking. What will need to be changed to overcome impending doom will be not something in the environment, or existence itself, but ourselves; and what is sacrificed in service of the wise king and mother nature will be good.

---

[128] See below for further exposition.

The inner battle of the psyche, between chaos and order, borne out in myth, provides the profound problem of life with a profound language. Peterson believes that we can't create our own values because values have evolved with us, the forms and structures by which we interpret the world in the first place, implicit in competence hierarchies, then articulated in our myths and, now, abstract concepts. He finds Plato's idea that all knowledge is remembrance true in a deep, even Darwinian, sense. We weren't merely born thirty years ago, but we're also the product of human language and history and over 12 billion years of evolution. We are descendants of the great heroes of the past. So Jung's idea is that we have to go back to the myths and extract the archetypes, in order to understand the forms the problem of suffering has taken, and the solutions presented by the victorious heroes and saviors of myth. Peterson's claims essentially boil down to making Jung's ideas more rational and articulate: "I'm trying to resurrect the dormant logos."

The Speech that Brings Novel Order to Chaos

"So what mediates between the domains of order and chaos? Consciousness, as far as I can tell. It's the hero, that's one way of thinking about it. It's the logos, that's another way of thinking about it. It's the word that generates order out of chaos at the beginning of time. It's the consciousness that's interacting with the matter of the world that produces

Being. That's basically it. That's basically you, for all intents and purposes."[129]

What is this logos? It is one of the oldest ideas and Peterson thinks its use in Christianity is particularly significant today. His interpretation of the logos may appear somewhat idiosyncratic, but it is highly instructive and, I think, a functional definition of the concept.

Jordan Peterson understands the logos to be the embodiment of the savior archetype, who is the mediator between order and chaos, and it means the ordering of the world by the manifestation of truth in speech.[130] When you enter a dark, unfamiliar room, with no light, what do you do? You grope in the dark until you find an object by which to orient yourself. Kant thought that this notion of orientation could be abstracted to thinking in general,[131] that thinking was an activity meant to orient ourselves in the world. Similarly, Peterson thinks telling the truth is the best way to orient ourselves when we are confronted by chaos, or "the unknown," the domain where the consequences of our actions are not self-evident and the situation in which we find ourselves has no obvious cause. Telling the truth situates us. "Chaos is transformed into order by the word…. If you want chaos to be turned into hell, then lie. If

---

[129] JRE, #958.

[130] Peterson traces a genealogy of the logos in his biblical lectures.

[131] What Does It Mean To Orient Oneself In Thinking?

you want chaos to be transformed into heaven, then tell the truth."[132]

Truth is fundamental for overcoming the problem of suffering. We have noted, already, that Peterson tells us to pay attention, because the very things we value the most might be the very things that cause us suffering (to hold onto our values, despite the appearance of the unknown, is functionally the notion of idolatry in Christianity).

> The truth is something that burns. It burns off deadwood, and people don't like having their deadwood burnt off; often because they're like 95% deadwood. Believe me, I'm not being snide about that. It's no joke. When you start to realize how much of what you've constructed of yourself is based on deception and lies, that is a horrifying realization, and it can easily be 95% of you.[133]

On another note, truth is the progenitor of the good. "The reality you bring out of potentiality with truth is good. That's one of the most profound discoveries of humanity."[134] How can this be so? Peterson believes he partly derived his understanding of truth from Nietzsche: "Truth is that which serves

---

[132] Stratford Festival, "The Productivity of War | The Forum | Stratford Festival 2014," YouTube, July 30, 2014, , accessed June 12, 2016, https://www.youtube.com/watch?v=6nX6fevCATI.

[133] JRE, #958.

[134] UTS, #46.

life."[135] The things that are most true are those which, over the years, have produced, sustained, and amplified life. This understanding of truth also makes sense of the claim that there is nothing truer than the archetypal ideas of religion: they are some of the oldest ideas we have. The form of argument is this: Those ideas which have served life are those ideas which have been trialed by evolution and proven true by existence. Peterson's question of truth is not merely whether a thing or proposition corresponds to reality, but whether the thing or proposition is true enough to serve life. We speak the truth in words, and thereby actualize potentiality by the truth, and it is necessarily good, because it will serve life rather than death, good over evil.

Words are very important to Peterson. We've evolved so that our ideas can die rather than ourselves or other people. We had to act out killing as will of God for millennia before we could abstractly derive this idea. "Myths of the fall and redemption portray the emergence of human dissatisfaction with present conditions—no matter how comfortable— and the tendency or desire for movement toward 'a better future.'"[136] Rather than being merely a tyrannical father, the realm of order, and the prevalence of tradition, can also be something like a wise king. You can bargain with reality, because what you encounter is partly the world and partly the abstract social system. This bargain takes the form of promises, sacrifices, exchanges of money, and the like.

---

[135] JRE, #958.

[136] Peterson, *Maps of Meaning*, 465.

Furthermore, that the future can be bargained with is a rational articulation of the deeper concept that the sacred is personal. One of the best comportments we can have toward tradition is to view it as something to be negotiated with, rather than as something that predetermines the future. "Through fire all things are renewed. And one of the deepest ideas of Christianity is that you should burn everything off that's part of you that isn't part of that thing that can die and be reborn."

The message of Jordan B. Peterson is no simplistic self-help guide: he does not think that life is simply good, nor does he think the journey to the good entails avoiding all which is evil or destroying something outside ourselves called "evil." Rather, the path to Heaven is like Jesus' journey to the wilderness: it requires confrontation with the monster, which means, functionally, to recognize your capacity for evil and control it. "If you understand who you are, then you understand Nazis. And who wants to understand Nazis?"[137] It's a frightening thing to realize that you're human, that you're responsible: to see both your tremendous potential to be good and your soul-snatching capacity to be evil.

This burden of consciousness confers responsibility to us (we see, here again, Herrmann's thoughts as a forerunner). We understand ourselves, for the first time, as actors, in control of the direction of our lives. One way out of this burden of consciousness it to return to naivete, to anesthetize self-reflection with drugs or to refuse to grow up, to depend on other people for self-validation for the rest

---

[137] JRE, #958.

of your life. Yet another way to deal with this burden is to become more conscious,[138] to, as it were, find life in it. Heighten your consciousness so that everything becomes integrated enough, the values from tradition that are still useful for the challenges of the future and the values of the future that demand changes of the past, so that this integration is its own medication.[139] To do this, you must stop avoiding terrible things, but confront them, which is the goal of psychotherapy: "Voluntary confrontation with what you're afraid of."[140] Also, pay attention, and what you will find will lead you to places you don't want to go, but they will be places that make you better and wiser, where you can acquire hard-won wisdom.[141] Wisdom allows us to deal honorably with the tragedy of life.

---

[138] In a different way, this is, famously, Albert Camus' solution to the problem of suicide: lucidity concerning the absurd.

[139] Peterson, "Reality and the Sacred."

[140] Peterson, "Reality and the Sacred."

[141] One difference between this heightened consciousness and, for instance, the kind of consciousness Buddhism advocates is that this kind of heightened consciousness isn't to show how everything is illusory, but to show that everything is in fact really real: the most basic reality is suffering, and to overcome suffering isn't to show how to become detached from everything, but to become really attached to them, and choose them, and say that no matter what happens this is good. It's more of a Albert Camus thing than a Sam Harris thing.

The purpose of life, as far as I can tell from studying mythology and from studying psychology for decades, is to find a mode of being that's so meaningful that the fact that life is suffering is no longer relevant; or maybe that it's even acceptable. I would say, as well, that people know when they are doing that. You know when you're doing that in part because you're no longer resentful. You say, 'Geez, I could do this forever.' There's a timelessness that's associated with that state of being. From a mythological perspective, that's equivalent to brief habitation of the Kingdom of God. It's the place so meaningful that it enables you to bear the harsh preconditions of life without becoming resentful, bitter, or cruel. And there's nothing that you can pursue in your life that will be half as useful as that.[142]

Humanity is torn between order and chaos, between the known and unknown, between the past and future. This is the basic situation to which we have adapted. And the fundamental framework for thinking about what it means to be human and for overcoming the basic problems of human existence is to look at how we have acted out the meaning of human existence through myth, and thereby discover the solutions we have developed for the problem

---

[142] We Plants Are Happy Plants, "The Purpose Of Life - Jordan Peterson," YouTube, December 22, 2016, accessed April 03, 2017, https://www.youtube.com/watch?v=F7DaMfneZhE&feature= youtu.be&t=177.

of suffering and articulate them as lucidly and truthfully as we can. Peterson's call to do so by situating religion and myth within a Darwinian framework is as novel as it is important.[143] This exploration of the subjectivizing influences on our systems of thought has shed new light on the meaning of religious symbols and their bearing on our day-to-day lives. In fact, the conclusions Jordan Peterson derives from the explication of myth amount to something like the ultimate balancing of subjective meaning with objective truth, selfishness and selflessness, facts and norms. "Personal interest—subjective meaning—reveals itself at the juncture of explored and unexplored territory, healthy individual and societal adaptation."[144] "Loyalty to personal interest is equivalent to identification with the archetypal hero."[145]

Telling the truth is a gamble on the benevolence of being. So the idea is you tell the truth, you don't manipulate the world to make it give you what you want, you try to articulate yourself—

---

[143] You can might what perspective toward religion is the most scientific, and Peterson answers that it is the Darwinian rather than the post-Enlightenment: whereas the Darwinian views religion as another systematic means of contending with our own subjectivity (as an evolutionary experiment concerning life), the post-Enlightenment, Peterson thinks, merely looks to taxonomize facts about religion and confuses the origins of religion with its effects. See for more on this #4 – Religion, Myth, Science, Truth.

[144] Peterson, *Maps of Meaning*, 447.

[145] Peterson, 447.

and articulate the manner of your being, as clearly and as comprehensively as possible— and then you see what happens.

And you decide—this is the act of faith—you decide that no matter what happens, if you tell the truth, that that's the best possible out- come.[146]

---

[146] The Rubin Report, "Jordan Peterson and Dave Rubin: Gender Pronouns and the Free Speech War (Full Interview)," YouTube, November 18, 2016, accessed November 20, 2016, https://www.youtube.com/watch?v=5n8zn-R10qM&feature=youtu.be&t=53m25s.

6. CULTURAL CONTROVERSIES: POSTMODERNISM, MARXISM, AND SPEECH LAWS

"There is something else going on. If there was-n't something else going on a relatively obscure professor's amateurish YouTube videos, on a relatively obscure piece of Canadian legislation, wouldn't have had any effect. It would have just disappeared. But it didn't. And that's because there's more going on than the straightforward issue surrounding the pronoun use."

Jordan Peterson, on the *Joe Rogan Experience*[147]

In this section, I want to turn to Peterson's political commitments. Peterson has become infamous and divisive for his political stances. Below I just want to describe how they follow, in part, from his thinking on philosophy and religion that predate our political moment, showing that he is not a simple reactionary, and his ideas deserve to be heard on their own merit, instead of being classified with the political opportunists of our day.

---

[147] JRE, #958.

Biographical Development

In his fourth podcast episode, "Religion, Myth, Science, Truth," Peterson walks us through the development of his political perspective. It began when he pursued his first degree in political science, because the causes of social conflict interested him. As he found that every explanation for social conflict was grounded in some kind of economic theory, placing resources (whether resource scarcity, resource production, etc.) as the central motivator for conflict, he became disenchanted with these dogmas in his studies. Because they didn't take into account the relation between belief and the individual, Peterson found these theories dubious.

Around this time (the second peak of the Cold War), he was obsessed with and terrified by the possibility of nuclear destruction. It all had just seemed gratuitous: that groups of people would inch closer to the potential annihilation of the human race for no apparent reason.[148] Peterson believed the

---

[148] There was a public demonstration of this phenomenon in the political science literature. It was described as "Mutually-Assured Destruction." The concept itself developed out of classical, realist foreign policy ideas. The basic concept was that if two countries had the capacity to destroy themselves and the world, and that capacity continued to grow, that the two countries wouldn't actually do it, for fear of destroying the human race. This is exactly what happened between the United States and the Soviet Union. While it seems irrational on the surface, there was deeply logical reasoning behind doing this, for if each country made the use of nuclear weapons impossible, the potential for peace was inevitable. Peterson's point would, I think, be that what is questionable is not, then, a realist-stand-off about the possibility of launching the nukes, but the creation of the nukes in the first place. What kind of

cause of this had to be deeper than the empirical level: it had to be metaphysical, relating to the embodied, motivational framework of our time. To make people as miserable as possible and to be counterproductive concerning your own ends, individually and politically, is just inconceivable without some kind of malevolent or irrational intent. The aims of the Cold War conflict seemed to be leveled against the possibility of being itself.

This malevolence, born of the irrational, was outlined by one of Peterson's heroes, a survivor of the USSR, the novelist Aleksandr Solzhenitsyn. He drew a connection between the lies individuals tell and the pathologies of the state.[149] Peterson felt that

---

drive would cause humans to create a weapon that could destroy everything, even if by accident? He has, in some places, pointed to our loss of the notion of truth as that which serves life to be part of the problem.

[149] "We shall be told: what can literature possibly do against the ruthless onslaught of open violence? But let us not forget that violence does not live alone and is not capable of living alone: it is necessarily interwoven with falsehood. Between them lies the most intimate, the deepest of natural bonds. Violence finds its only refuge in falsehood, falsehood its only support in violence. Any man who has once acclaimed violence as his METHOD must inexorably choose falsehood as his PRINCIPLE. At its birth violence acts openly and even with pride. But no sooner does it become strong, firmly established, than it senses the rarefaction of the air around it and it cannot continue to exist without descending into a fog of lies, clothing them in sweet talk. It does not always, not necessarily, openly throttle the throat, more often it demands from its subjects only an oath of allegiance to falsehood, only complicity in falsehood." From Aleksandr Solzhenitsyn's Nobel Prize Speech 1970

he needed to examine himself to determine if there were actions he had taken and beliefs he subscribed to which contributed to this situation. Indeed, as an individual placed within a broader society who saw the arrival of the Cold War, it was more likely than not that he reflected this environment in some way. Psychologist Sigmund Freud, another hero, theorized that pathologies in individuals were caused by repressions, which are, for Peterson, forms of lying. It's not just rational elements that drive people to war, as a result. There is something deeper, and irrational. What lies were we telling ourselves that caused the Cold War?

The social ills of society are in part explained by the stripping of subjectivity from the world, for this erasure causes us to lie about what we're actually doing, what we're actually aiming at. This is the lie: that the world is best conceptualized as simple objects in relation to each other, stripped from the context of the forces of life. As we abstract from embodied narratives that give meaning to our beliefs, and turn our gaze toward the beliefs themselves as the progenitor of meaning, we become more disconnected from the grammar of these beliefs, causing a "forgetfulness of Being,"[150] or the appearance of groundless values. The forgetfulness of Being is not an innocent development. It's the appearance of

---

[150] See this very brief but immensely articulate exposition of Martin Heidegger's famous idea, which, consequently, mirrors Peterson's ideas in many ways: David E. Cooper, "Martin Heidegger: The Forgetfulness of Being – TheTLS," TheTLS, September 14, 2018, , accessed November 08, 2018, https://www.the-tls.co.uk/articles/public/heidegger-forgetfulness-being/.

the lie that we do not owe, and are not still indebted to, religious myth, for we mistake those values[151] that have produced meaningful concepts with the concepts themselves, thereby repressing the grounds from which our philosophical, political, and religious systems were birthed.

When values are groundless, we believe we can create any values we want. This in effect is the second lie: our ideas are correlated to conscious belief, and, completely abstracted from the unconscious domain, we are told we can change anything in the world so long as we work together. What if this causes us to suffer? What if, indeed, we find that the traditional social structures are more apt to minimize suffering and maximize cooperation and flourishing? Today we are told this is inconceivable: we must only work more diligently toward the ends laid out by our abstracted systems of beliefs which, by definition, disregard biological, historical, and social forces. As the repression (and absence) of truthful speech which orders our intentions is replaced with a concealing of intentions—for our intentions, we are told, can only be understood with reference to orthodox doctrine of enforced ideology—a race to obtain objective group goods that confer hierarchical status by any means necessary becomes a form of value itself. What follows from this, which is what our present situation is perhaps on a trajectory toward, is either nihilism or totalitarianism, where all meaning is nonexistent or completely objective. In a "perfect" society, to acquire socially

---

[151] More exactly put values here means "metaphysical substructure" or "a priori framework."

desirable status and material goods is, by definition, to live a good life. To suffer in this situation is to be illegitimate. Is there a suffering that goes beyond material possession and social group identity? Yes, and we repress it, lie to ourselves about it, in our pursuit of group status. This is the problem Peterson confronts and for which he aims to provide an antidote.[152]

Postmodernism and Marxism

Although Peterson receives a lot of flak for his use of the term "postmodernism," what he means by it actually coheres with the definition in Encyclopedia Britannica: "a late 20th-century movement characterized by broad skepticism, subjectivism, or relativism; a general suspicion of reason; and an acute sensitivity to the role of ideology in asserting and maintaining political and economic power."[153] This is what he means by postmodernism, and he has said as much.[154] Many friends I have, and many online commentators, disparage Peterson for not adequately engaging with Postmodern thinkers in writing such as Derrida or Foucault. Whereas I agree with their basic points, and think Peterson is not as far away from these thinkers as he believes

---

[152] We have already seen his solution: find that way of being which makes suffering, not only justified, but beside the point. Find meaning.

[153] Brian Duignan, "Postmodernism," Encyclopædia Britannica, October 25, 2018,
https://www.britannica.com/topic/postmodernism-philosophy.

[154] See JRE, #958, in particular.

he is, the fact still remains that people he engages with, who show up to protest his speeches and events, hold the positions he calls "postmodern," and this fact perhaps outweighs, though does not exonerate, Peterson's lack of academic critique of serious postmodern thinkers. He does not need to be a scholar of Derrida or Foucault or Deleuze to use "postmodernism" descriptively and to say something meaningful about it. We can distinguish between postmodernism as a family of philosophical traditions, as a social condition, and as a popular set of ideological movements and impulses. What Peterson is responding to are the last two categories of postmodernism. And to the extent that he is responsible for mischaracterizing the first, I think, bears no relevance on whether his critiques of the last two categories are valid.

Yet, he has not kept entirely silent on postmodern thinkers, as one of his most in-depth expositions of postmodernism comes by way of Derrida in his discussion with Joe Rogan.[155] The basic narrative Peterson tells is this: Jacques Derrida is the central villain of postmodernism. A Marxist to begin with, as Marxism fell out of favor in the 1970s, when no intellectual could deny its evil deeds, he shifted his Marxism and began playing identity politics, grounding the Marxist oppressor/oppressed conflict on identity rather than on economic divisions. The way Derrida did this was to focus his philosophical project on the framing problem: the recognition that there are an infinite number of ways to interpret a finite set of objects, which means there are an infi-

---

[155] JRE, #958.

nite number of ways to interpret a text, which means the world is subject to an infinite number of interpretations as well. What follows is the claim that there is no right or correct way to interpret the world. From this claim, Derrida concludes that those who have interpreted the world do so in a way that facilitates acquisition of power. Thus, we get identity politics: All people do is play power games based on their identities.

As we can see, Peterson's equation for marrying postmodernism with Marxism is relatively simple. On the empirical level, people who show up at protests against him carry the clean, commodified hammer and sickle flag.[156] On the theoretical level, Peterson believes people who make claims of group identity do so under the influence of a latent, ideological Marxism. According to Peterson, those who have fallen prey to the postmodern ethos do not believe in dialogue with those they oppose because dialogue, like all else, is grounded in power. Claims of truth are, as a result, claims to power: to control the narrative about what truth is.

He has, since I wrote this, outlined as much in an article published on his website.[157] This is not such a tidy marriage, he admits. Theoretically, the

---

[156] JRE, #958.

[157] Jordan B. Peterson, "Postmodernism: Definition and Critique (with a Few Comments on Its Relationship with Marxism)," Jordan Peterson, May 28, 2018, accessed June 02, 2018, https://jordanbpeterson.com/philosophy/postmodernism-definition-and-critique-with-a-few-comments-on-its-relationship-with-marxism/.

postmodern skepticism toward grand narrative does not cohere with the Marxist dialectical materialist claims about history and the future, but practically the two are intermingled in an incoherent morass, which, indeed, is part of the pathology.

Peterson thinks postmodern Marxists are wrong because what you extract from the world is a game you can play. From the things we encounter in the world and the values we contend with in the social sphere we extract a set of tools, so that we don't suffer too much and people will cooperate with us in sustainable and reciprocal ways. The best functional aim is to live and thrive in multiple environments among multiple people. And Peterson thinks these are actual constraints on interpretations. From his Darwinian perspective, Peterson believes Marxism forgets the evolutionary structures which have, before our politics could even develop, regulated the ways in which we relate to each other.

The major issue Peterson has with postmodernism, then, is that it aims to destroy what he believes we have gained from millennia of trial and error: the metaphysical and ethical substructure that grounds our social values derived from myths. Whereas the ethical substructure based on myth aims at, for the most part, solving the problem of suffering by presenting a turning inward as its solution,[158] political ideologies that interpret every ethic as a power game relegate the problem of suffering, and therefore its solution, to an outward phenome-

---

[158] See Kierkegaard, who presents the very same solution, in *The Present Age: On the Death of Rebellion* and *Purity of Heart is to Will One Thing*.

non: the state. If we lose the concept of truth to its reduction by power, or the possibility of discourse to its reduction by identity, then we lose what we gained from the distillation of the Enlightenment: rationality, empiricism, science, clarity of mind, dialogue, and the individual. Why speak the truth if it might offend: why not proceed by a lie and construct the perfect state with ends that will justify the means, even if these means are never actualized? Why tell the truth if a lie will make the masses feel better momentarily while we work on the perfect organization of society? Hannah Arendt's answer is very close to Peterson's:

> The more people's standpoints I have present in my mind while I am pondering a given issue, and the better I can imagine how I would feel and think if I were in their place, the stronger will be my capacity for representative thinking and the more valid my final conclusions, my opinion. (It is this capacity for an 'enlarged mentality' that enables man to judge…. The very process of opinion formation is determined by those in whose places somebody thinks and uses his own mind, and the only condition for this exertion of the imagination is disinterestedness, the liberation from one's own private interests.[159]

---

[159] Hannah Arendt, *The Portable Hannah* Arendt (New York: Penguin Books, 2003), 556.

The only way to obtain this "impartiality," which means the liberation from fixation on one's private interests, is to tell the truth, to be honest with oneself: "truth and truthfulness have always constituted the highest criterion of speech and endeavor."[160] Lying, on the other hand, simplifies the world into basic images, as in political propaganda which says there is one simple solution and one simple problem and if you don't stand on the side of the good then you are evil. Ideology inhibits us from both empathy and thinking. This is precisely Peterson's point, and, he believes, the rejection of science and myth amounts to the victory of the lie and of the state over the truth and the individual.

If you think this is too far, Peterson has debated with a professor of Transgender Studies who claimed "it's not correct that there is such a thing as biological sex."[161] Many think Peterson uses hyperbole to heighten the stakes of his claims unrealistically. But for those who have followed a least a small percentage of his interactions with his critics, what are at stake do indeed appear to be the values of the Enlightenment itself.[162]

---

[160] Arendt, 571.

[161] The Agenda with Steve Paikin, "Genders, Rights and Freedom of Speech," YouTube, October 26, 2016, accessed November 10, 2016,
https://www.youtube.com/watch?v=kasiov0ytEc.

[162] See the case of Evergreen College for an example. Jonathan Haidt has written on this topic as well.

Hierarchies Revisited: How Inequality is Created in the Pursuit of Value

In his Oxford Union Address,[163] Peterson outlines the development of hierarchies and values in a way I had not heard him argue before. It is instructive here to outline this argument, as it will contribute to an understanding of his reasons for rejecting postmodernism on Darwinian grounds.

A fundamental characteristic of biological organisms is that they must move forward, toward those things that satiate biological needs and away from those things that render life impossible. This encapsulates two basic motivational drives: approach and avoidance. Yet, as people, we are not motivated simply to fulfill biological needs or avoid natural predators; we desire and move toward those things that make life worth living in the first place. We seek not just the maintenance of life but the grandeur, the beauty, and the meaning of life. And it's these things which make life worth living that we *value*. Therefore, as humans, we always live within a framework of value, composed both of biological and psychological necessity.

Because we have to move, to achieve the fulfillment of a need like hunger or a goal like a promotion at a job, the present, the place we are in right now, is hardly ever the best place to be. There could be a predator nearby, we might be suffering from hunger pangs, or the place we are at in the so-

---

[163] Jordan B. Peterson, "Oxford Union Full Address and Q&A Transcript," Jordan Peterson, September 25, 2018, , accessed October 02, 2018,
https://jordanbpeterson.com/transcripts/oxford-union/.

cial hierarchy might make us depressed. We're always thinking ahead, projecting, fantasizing, planning.[164]

Furthermore, as humans, we pursue these goals, and recognize these values, in *social* spaces, because we are social creatures. We have to "compete and cooperate" with other people to pursue values. We can reason from this that all things valuable are pursued within a social context and the pursuit of value occurs as a "social enterprise." Hierarchies of competence are generated because of these pursuits, as some people will prove more skillful or intelligent depending on what values are pursued at any given time. By implication, a certain portion of the population will have a tremendous amount of success whereas others will fail or comparatively underperform. "It's an iron law of the distribution of success and hierarchies. So if you're going to have value and you're going to have hierarchy, then

---

[164] As a side note, it should be remembered the connection with suffering here: Once we have achieved satiation, we find a new place to move toward, a new goal to pursue. Yet it is also always possible that the future we move toward will not be actualized, even if we take all the necessary precautions and have all the required skills to achieve our goals. In this regard, it turns out that a fundamental condition of life is suffering: We often fail, we're often crushed by circumstances outside our control, we're often blamed for things we didn't do or accused of intentions we don't recognize as our own. For Peterson, it is the pursuit of value that gives life meaning despite suffering, as he quotes Nietzsche, "he who has a why can bear any how."

you're going to have inequality. That's a problem."[165]

Peterson understands the differences between liberals and conservatives to be centered on this problem. Conservatives, in attempting to conserve tradition, are motivated by preserving the hierarchies that have endured through time. Preservation of the hierarchy is in some sense tantamount to the preservation of the pursuit of values that generated the hierarchies in the first place. The destruction of hierarchy in general means the destruction of value itself; yet in this framework, it's an untenable position. Here, we might think, conservatives have a point.

Liberals are not however concerned with the destruction of hierarchy, but rather with "inequality of distribution" and corruption that hierarchies naturally trend toward. A hierarchy that produces extreme inequality is unstable, because those who have nothing have nothing to lose and, even to the destruction of the hierarchy itself, may desire to exact revenge on those who have everything. Similarly, "once a hierarchy of competence has been established, it can be invaded by people who use power as the means to attain status in the hierarchy."[166]

Peterson believes we need both conservatives and liberals for a functioning democracy: conservatives to maintain and regulate hierarchies and liberals to establish new values around which hierarchies form. We should not lie either about the possibility

---

[165] Peterson, "Oxford Union."

[166] Peterson, "Oxford Union."

of hierarchical entropy nor about hierarchical necessity. To do so misunderstands how values originate and endure through time.

One question he has been asking repeatedly in regards to liberal politics is how do we know when liberal politics have gone too far in its attempt to establish new values?[167] From history, and the laws instituted because of this history in the West, we know when conservatives have gone too far in their attempt to preserve hierarchies: when they exclude people based on skin color or race. But, for Peterson, the West has not learned from the brutality of communism, and so liberals have not yet drawn the line it should not cross. One line that should not be crossed, Peterson believes, is the doctrine of equality of outcome.[168] We see this today in HR departments that push for *equity*: the demand that a percentage of employees reflect a representative percentage of the population. When, against biological, psychological, historical, and scientific facts, it demands equal distribution of credit obtained from a

---

[167] See Jordan B. Peterson, "The Moral Obligation of the Moderate Leftists," Jordan Peterson, April 12, 2018, accessed April 15, 2018,
https://jordanbpeterson.com/uncategorized/the-moral-obligation-of-the-moderate-leftists/. For an extended discussion of this point, see the infamous Jordan B. Peterson, "Political Correctness: A Force for Good? A Munk Debate," YouTube, May 20, 2018, , accessed May 20, 2018, https://www.youtube.com/watch?v=ST6kj9OEYf0.

[168] See the transcript here:
https://www.aspenideas.org/sites/default/files/Jordan%20Peterson%20From%20the%20Barricades%20of%20the%20Culture%20Wars.pdf.

hierarchy for all members of the hierarchy, even those who are underperformers and charlatans, then liberals have gone too far. A particular issue with this doctrine is it "tribalizes our perceptions," dividing populations by shallow traits, such as skin color or gender identity, rather than deeper traits, such as merit. Who, in effect, measures equality of outcome, who chooses who measures it, which identities are measured, and what are the dimensions of equality measured, just economic?[169] The probability that this leads to the horrific atrocities that it did in the USSR, for Peterson, is high. Again, this is why the basic unit of a democratic society is not the group but the individual, and the laws presently tend to reflect this idea. Individuals are the most complex entities, and choosing protections for individuals is the best approximation for achieving liberty and justice for all. Whereas equality of opportunity is just and should be pursued, equality of outcome, in Peterson's estimation, is reprehensible.

Peterson's rejection of what he calls postmodern Marxist propaganda, especially as it is instituted today in liberal discourse, is a rejection of its claims that all hierarchies are hierarchies of power and a rejection of its doctrine of equality of outcome. Rather than attempting to change society by legislating change according to the dogma of the day, Peterson is interested in understanding not only how pathologies of group identity cause social instability, but also how these pathologies are grounded in the experiences of individuals. He wants us to look at our-

---

[169] See, again, The Big Think commentary https://www.youtube.com/watch?v=8UVUnUnWfHI.

selves in the mirror before we look out onto the world, projecting our insecurities, ill-conceived notions, and pathologies onto the landscape. And he wants us to do so by remaining honest with ourselves, telling the truth, and examining our good intentions for their possible catastrophic consequences. It just might be the case that those structures passed along by tradition may permeate deeper into our psyches than any idealized world does.

A Final Return to the Christian Myth

Peterson is infamous for his love-affair with the Christian myth. One reason for this is that he thinks the story on which western civilization is founded is the Christian myth. This claim bears some explanation, as its importance is not entirely apparent today. Jacques Ellul has noted[170] that Christianity differs from religions that came before it because it did not rise with a culture, but came to fruition within already developed Roman and Jewish cultures. Christianity was used in turn to explicitly shape and order the societies that followed it. It was a reversal of the historical marrying of culture and religion, placing the latter before the former chronologically.

So what does it mean, particularly considering the chronological note we have made, that Christianity is the story on which western civilization is founded? This is a primary claim of Peterson's, following in part from his conception of the origin of religion and his awareness of history. He means this quite literally. The story of the Old Testament, he

---

[170] Jacques Ellul, *The New Demons*.

thinks, the interpretation of which he gets from Northrop Frye, is that the solution to suffering is the construction of the perfect state. But the New Testament answers differently, placing the individual as the site of salvation: the individual that tells the truth, who is the incarnation of the logos. And it is this Christian insight on which the West stands.

This is, in effect, the summation of Peterson's politics: How are you going to change the world when you can't even keep your room clean? Fundamentally, his challenge is to not perpetuate your pathologies socially by participating in politics as a means to overcome your suffering, but first get yourself in order.[171] He believes with Jung that "...if

---

[171] He gives an especially helpful summary of his political position in the interview above:
So I guess that's what I'd ask: "just think it through. We're tribalizing our perceptions. Can you think of any ways that might not work out so well? How would you mitigate against that?" One of the reasons that I'm a traditionalist, let's say— because I'm not really temperamentally suited for being conservative, despite the fact that I've identified as the only extant right-wing psychologist. That was a joke, primarily. It's because one of the things that wise social scientists know and attempt to transmit to their students is, "the probability that your well-meaning intervention"—say, at a clinical level or an epidemiological level—"will have the positive outcome you intend and no other is zero. In fact, the highest probability is that it will kickback against you and make things worse. So you bloody well better be sure when you implement your well-intentioned intervention that you lay out a measurement strategy to determine what the consequences of that intervention are, because they're very unlikely to be an improvement." That's especially the case if the system is already working well, because if it's already at 85 per cent optimal capacity,

the individual is not truly regenerated in spirit, society cannot be either, for society is the sum total of individuals in need of redemption."[172]   And he doesn't think postmodernism allows for this kind of ordering and, rather, subjects the individual to the tyranny of ideology. Why tell the truth, anyway, if by the truth we offend another, or discover physical limitations to idealized harmonies we aim for in our utopian visions of the state? Why tell the truth when truthful speech can be violent?[173]

---

moving it up another 5 per cent is really hard, whereas making it 50 per cent worse—any fool can manage that.

So when things are working, be very cautious about what you do radically to fix them, because you don't know what the consequence of your intervention is going to be. That's another thing that I might suggest: caution. And to the degree that I'm a conservative, I'm a conservative because of my apprehension of my own ignorance. It's like, "first, do no harm." That's also why, in my public lectures, I council people, let's say, to put their own house in order. You're not going to hurt anyone by doing that. All it's going to do is make you a little less chaotic and horrible. And then, maybe you'll be of a little more benefit to your family. That might be a nice thing, too. And then, maybe you could dare to extend a tentacle out beyond that and tap something in the real world gently. Well, that isn't what we're taught in universities. We're taught, "well, you're eighteen, and you can see what's wrong, and you should think up some ways of radically transforming the economic system." Right.

[172] C. G. Jung, *The Undiscovered Self* (Signet: 2006), 56.

[173] Lisa Feldman Barrett, "When Is Speech Violence?" The New York Times, July 15, 2017, , accessed July 20, 2017, https://www.nytimes.com/2017/07/14/opinion/sunday/when-is-speech-violence.html.

I recommend everyone who wants a basic understanding of the thrust of Peterson's politics to read C. G. Jung's very accessible and very brief work *The Undiscovered Self: The Dilemma of the Individual in Modern Society*. There one will find the beating heart of Peterson's political faith and the monsters he hopes to fend off:

> In order to free the fiction of the sovereign state—in other words, the whims of those who manipulate it—from every wholesome restriction, all socio-political movements tending in this direction invariably try to cut the ground from under the religions. For, in order to turn the individual into a function of the State, his dependence on anything beside the State must be taken from him. But religion means dependence on and submission to the irrational facts of experience. These do not refer directly to social and physical conditions; they concern far more the individual's psychic attitude.[174]

We can immediately see the parallel in this indictment with Peterson's. Religion for Jung does not mean institutionalized rituals or holy sites, but it means the individual's relationship to a superordinate principle that sits outside everyday contingencies and orders life and its circumstances by its compelling force. This is the same for Peterson, especially the notion of "God." Whereas if when religion (in this technical sense) wanes, political fanaticism intensifies, it follows that a regrounding in re-

---

[174] Jung, 19.

ligion protects against the onslaught of totalitarianism or nihilism which institutes the state as the superordinate principle. Many more people than Peterson have arrived at this conclusion, and it warrants some serious reflection. It is not a stretch to think that when he spoke out against Bill C-16, effectively standing up for "free speech," Peterson understood himself to be in the circumstances Jung described some half-century ago:

> The State has taken the place of God....But the religious function cannot be dislocated and falsified in this way without giving rise to secret doubts, which are immediately repressed so as to avoid conflict with the prevailing trends towards mass-mindedness. The result, as always in such cases, is overcompensation in the form of fanaticism, which in its turn is used as a weapon for stamping out the least flicker of opposition. Free opinion is stifled and moral decision ruthlessly suppressed, on the plea that the end justifies the means, even the vilest. The policy of the State is exalted to a creed, the leader or party boss becomes a demigod beyond good and evil, and his votaries are honored as heroes, martyrs, apostles, missionaries. There is only one truth and beside it no other. It is sacrosanct and above criticism. Anyone who thinks differently is a heretic, who, as we know from history, is threatened with all manner of unpleasant things. Only the party boss, who holds the political power in his hands, can interpret the State

doctrine authentically, and he does so just as suits him.[175]

Peterson's popularity came about initially with his criticism of Bill C-16,[176] spread across a series of protracted YouTube videos. His main contentions circled around (1) the idea that the law required the recognition of nonscientific positions as factual truth, effectively legislating truth by political power, and (2) compelled speech.[177, 178] On the first issue, Peterson has said the bill rests on the claim that there is no biological basis for gender identity, gender expression, and sex: that they vary independently, though these three are correlated upwards of .95.[179] The second issue of compelled speech is important to Peterson for a few reasons: (1) he's not "willing to cede linguistic territory to

---

[175] Jung, 23-24.

[176]https://en.wikipedia.org/wiki/An_Act_to_amend_the_Canadian_Human_Rights_Act_and_the_Criminal_Code

[177] See Peterson's Senate hearing regarding these issues here: Jordan B. Peterson, "2017/05/17: Senate Hearing on Bill C16," YouTube, May 18, 2017, accessed May 20, 2017, https://www.youtube.com/watch?v=KnIAAkSNtqo.

[178] For a commentary on Peterson's views of C-16 in particular, see Lisa Cumming, "Are Jordan Peterson's Claims About Bill C-16 Correct?" Torontoist, December 19, 2016, , accessed February 05, 2017, https://torontoist.com/2016/12/are-jordan-petersons-claims-about-bill-c-16-correct/. My aim here is to simply outline how these views are simply instantiations of his overall philosophical project about the problem of suffering and its solution.

[179] He makes this claim in JRE, #958.

postmodern radicals;" (2) he doesn't accept that those who have spoken on behalf of LGBTQI people politically represent them, since there have been no elections; and (3) he doesn't believe legislating compelled speech is democratic. None of this means, however, that he's unwilling to accept the reality that some people are in fact LGBTQI, or that he'd refuse to use the pronoun such persons prefer.[180]

His intentions, far from being parochial or regressive, are easily understood when placed within the context of his own work, alongside Jung and others. The world that science discovered was an achievement, because it allowed us to become more objective by separating judgements of meaning from judgments of fact. When the two are muddied, once again, we have an undermining of the hierarchy and values that produced the distinction in the first place: the mythical substructure in which democracy has its home. On a different note the question is still relevant: how, indeed, have these "leaders" of the LGBTQI "community" become spokespeople for the community in the first place? For Peterson, it appears that the competence hierarchies put in place to galvanize democracy are being manipulated by people who have no competence but have a lot of power and the desire to gain status. It

---

[180] Although he has said this many times over, he has said it recently on The Rubin Report, "Jordan Peterson and Ben Shapiro: Frontline of Free Speech (LIVE)," YouTube, January 31, 2018, , accessed February 01, 2018, https://www.youtube.com/watch?v=iRPDGEgaATU.

is an open question, anyway. And he provides examples that seem to support his suspicion.[181,182,183]

---

[181] Rogan, 958.

[182] See also his conversation with Camille Paglia where
he connects the postmodern motive with resentment:
https://jordanbpeterson.com/transcripts/camille-paglia/.

[183] See also his recent commentary on Durham City's
Council's public denouncement of his book tour: Jordan B.
Peterson, "Durham City Council Purchases Unearned Virtue
with the Currency of Denouncement," Jordan Peterson, July
09, 2018, , accessed August 02, 2018,
https://jordanbpeterson.com/political-correctness/durham-city-
council-purchases-unearned-virtue-with-the-currency-of-
denouncement/.

7. FINAL REMARKS

"What can I not doubt? The reality of suffering. It brooks no arguments. Nihilists cannot undermine it with skepticism. Totalitarians cannot banish it. Cynics cannot escape from its reality. Suffering is real, and the artful infliction of suffering on another, for its own sake, is wrong. That became the cornerstone of my belief. Searching through the lowest reaches of human thought and action, understanding my own capacity to act like a Nazi prison guard or a gulag archipelago trustee or a torturer of children in a dungeon, I grasped what it meant to 'take the sins of the world onto oneself.' Each human being has an immense capacity for evil. Each human being understands, a priori*, perhaps not what is good, but certainly what is not. And if there is something that* is not good*, then there is something that* is good*. If the worst sin is the torment of others, merely for the sake of the suffering produced—then the good is whatever diametrically opposed to that."*

Jordan B. Peterson, *12 Rules for Life: An Antidote to Chaos*[184]

---

[184] Jordan B. Peterson, *12 Rules for Life: An Antidote to Chaos* (Toronto: Random House Canada, 2018), 197-198.

As we explored Peterson's work from philosophy to science, religion to politics, it has become clear that his ideas—developed long before the time-specific scandals and controversies of the last few years—are not articulated out of mere political opportunism or the desire for fame. We still might ask if our discourses have yet gained anything by the inclusion of his voice? What are the contributions of Jordan B. Peterson? This, in part, is bound up with the background question of this book: Why tell the truth?

Earlier, we argued that Peterson has, if not reintroduced, revitalized pragmatism in the public square. What this has brought about is a re-evaluation of the role of religion in secular society. Whereas only the doctrinal content of religious belief was predominately the focus of critiques of religion in the recent past, Jordan Peterson has raised the possibility that religion might be aiming at something other than a scientific theory of the world, and it may just be the key to a meaningful life despite suffering and the antidote to the pathology of ideological possession. Similarly, from integrating pragmatism with Darwinism, he has come out against the view of humans as primarily rational creatures, suggesting that there is more to our motivational framework than meets the eye, and in fact much of it may be driven by unconscious forces. What this means is that we are not entirely transparent to ourselves, and that the beliefs we articulate as fundamental to our action or social life may in fact be incorrect or, at least, misrepresentative of our motivational frameworks as a whole. If Peterson is right that our beliefs are embodied before they are codified in articulated speech, and that religious myth might be the grammar of story itself—the medium for the communication of belief—then we have to be very careful about the stories we tell ourselves, about the stories we disregard, and about the role, whether conscious or unconscious, such stories play in our everyday lives. This begs, of course, a re-evaluation of the role of religion in secular society.

To go alongside his theories on philosophy and science stand his political commitments. What are we to make of them, as he is at once accused of being a prophet of the Alt-Right while himself criticizing this group?[185] We are mistaken if we separate his political critiques from his philosophy and religious ideas, as the turmoil and angst of the late Cold War introduced the problem of group identity and belief to Peterson in the first place, and in political terms. Beliefs appear to be essential to human identity yet inevitably come into conflict over time. Asking whether there is any escape from this loop of pathology and violence, Peterson finally arrived at the individual, and that telling the truth and being responsible for oneself diminishes dependency on ideological doctrines to give life meaning and shape society. What if, he asks, we, rather than looking for

---

[185] See his blog post "On the so-called 'Jewish Question'" found on his website: Jordan B. Peterson, "On the So-called "Jewish Question"," Jordan Peterson, April 25, 2018, accessed April 28, 2018, https://jordanbpeterson.com/psychology/on-the-so-called-jewish-question/.

villains around us, look at the evil of what we are capable? What if we live up to the demands of life right now, whether life demands at this point suffering or grand challenges, and do courageously and vigorously? What if rather than going out to change the world we first make our beds, paying attention to the things around us we can control and the relationships with others we can shape to become better and wiser? His politics, in sum, is perhaps best expressed this way:

> His insight here parallels those of Rene Girard and other anthropologists who point out that the only way of stopping unconscious sacrifice to blind gods (which is what happened in the atrocities of Hitler and what happens in our own bitter slandering of others) is through self-sacrifice. Only when we accept at the cost of personal suffering our own contingencies, sin, and mortality will we stop projecting these on to others so to make them suffer in order to feel better about ourselves.[186]

In our cultural moment, when questions of the relation between speech and violence, of the identification of political ends with group identity, of the culture of groundless cynicism, partisanship, and suspicion of online tribal communities, bolstered by platform algorithms aimed at stimulation over healthy *relation*, it seems Peterson's contribution can be boiled down to the appeal to examine first

---

[186]https://www.thebostonpilot.com/opinion/article.asp?ID=183427.

our own ideas, our own relationship to ourselves, and our own misdeeds and blasphemies before we begin to criticize others for theirs. This is no mere political fatalism or, conversely, quietism. Whereas our educational systems prize the amalgamation of factual information over *thinking*, the radical resides in the seemingly useless. Despite the moralism attached to turning inward, we are told from all corners of the earth that our world is in crisis, and to buck the demand to engage in actions that yield immediate consequences in order to examine ourselves is, by all political logic, unjustifiable. To be quiet, by the logic of immediacy and efficiency, is to endorse or be complicit with the worst of our time.

> Taking the easy way out or telling the truth—those are not merely two different choices. They are different pathways through life. They are utterly different ways of existing.
> You can use words to manipulate the world into delivering what you want. This is what it means to 'act politically.'[187]

It is no postmodern Marxism that is Peterson's bogeyman, it is rather *deceit*. When we experience suffering in the world, when we pay attention to our own vulnerabilities, then it is those who lie to themselves, who, from the experience of failure, take as their lesson that it is not their fault, it is not their knowledge that is incomplete or their values that are misguided, but the world's, and to exact revenge on

---

[187] Peterson, *12 Rules*, 209.

the world for the suffering inherent in existence is to live out the lie. He finds this not only in the archetype of Satan, but, from Solzhenitsyn's guidance, the Soviet citizenry: "the almost universal proclivity of the Soviet citizen to falsify his own day-to-day personal experience, deny his own state-induced suffering, and thereby prop up the dictates of the rational, ideology-possessed communist system."[188]

Postmodern Marxism is, for Peterson, the ideological lie the liberal spirit in the West is tempted by today. For Peterson, it is the lie that there are no hierarchies of competence (only dominance); the lie that biology and gender are not interdependent; the lie that group identity is more primary than the individual; the lie that there are no constraints to interpretation; the lie that the success of elites is a consequence of privilege rather than competence; the lie that good intentions lead to good outcomes; the lie that we can create our own values; the lie that religion is a poison. This is not to say that any of these issues are simple, or that the opposite of the propositions above are just unproblematically true. To "manipulate the world into delivering what you want" guides the rational ego, and it is not inherently pernicious. But to want what cannot *sustain* life, to aim at it, is to live the lie. Peterson does not want to sacrifice speaking the truth for what he considers to be a lie, even if that entails telling someone what they do not want to hear: the little lies we tell to keep the peace are perhaps the necessary preconditions for the social lie (like Stalinism or Nazism) to

---

[188] Peterson, 215.

appear. We either shape ourselves to become the people who tell the truth, and so shape reality by speaking the truth, or to tell the lie, and so disfigure everything in our own demonic image. The question of truth for Peterson is not merely a question of getting the facts straight, but also a question of what it means to be authentically human.

So why tell the truth? One reason is practical: "If you bend everything totally, blindly and willfully towards the attainment of a goal, and only that goal, you will never be able to discover if another goal would serve you, and the world, better. It is this that you sacrifice if you do not tell the truth."[189] Another is more existential. Peterson thinks that if we are honest with ourselves, make our own goals, values, and ideas lucid to ourselves, then when tragedy occurs or evil is endured then we will not die because of it: telling the truth keeps us grounded. It allows us to transcend any particular game, any particular moment in which we find ourselves, to embody qualities that allow us to succeed and live across all sets of games across time. As Peterson writes,

> Everyone needs a concrete, specific goal—an ambition, and a purpose—to limit chaos and make intelligible sense of his or her life. But all such concrete goals can and should be subordinated to what might be considered a meta-goal, which is a way of approaching and formulating

---

[189] Peterson, 225.

goals themselves. The meta-goal could be 'live in truth.'[190]

And so, we end where we began. The technologies that diminish our capacities to think can be manipulated for other ends: Jordan Peterson's popularity has skyrocketed, and his videos and interviews are being noticed by more and more people. Indeed, we might call this "The Jordan Peterson Moment."191 As a thinker, he sits firmly within the philosophical traditions spurred by Nietzsche, William James, and Jung. And as an influence, he's a cultural force that we will not soon forget. Why tell the truth in our age of group-think and Twitter epigrams? Well, it's our only hope for survival, and the only way for the hero, who speaks a freeing word that organizes chaos into novel order, to emerge. As Peterson concludes in *Maps of Meaning:*

The point of our limitations is not suffering; it is existence itself. We have been granted the capacity to voluntarily bear the terrible weight of our mortality. We turn from that capacity and degrade ourselves because we are afraid of responsibility. In this manner, the necessarily tragic preconditions of existence are made intolerable.

---

[190] Peterson, 226-227.

[191] Brooks, David. "The Jordan Peterson Moment." The New York Times. January 26, 2018. Accessed November 08, 2018. https://www.nytimes.com/2018/01/25/opinion/jordan-peterson-moment.html.

It seems to me that it is not the earthquake, the flood or the cancer that makes life unbearable, horrible as those events appear. We seem capable of withstanding natural disaster, even of responding to that disaster in an honorable and decent manner. It is rather the pointless suffering that we inflict upon each other—our evil—that makes life appear corrupt beyond acceptability; that undermines our ability to manifest faith in our central natures. So why should the capacity for evil exist?. . . But how can we put an end to our errors? What path can we follow to eliminate our blindness and stupidity, to bring us closer to the light? Christ said, Be ye therefore perfect, as your Father in heaven is perfect. But how? We seem stymied, as always, by Pontius Pilate's ironic query: What is truth? (John 18:38)

Well, even if we don't know precisely what the truth is, we can certainly tell, each of us, what it isn't. It isn't greed, and the desire, above all else, for constant material gain; it isn't denial of experience we know full well to be real, and the infliction of suffering for the purpose of suffering. Perhaps it is possible to stop doing those things which we know, beyond doubt, to be wrong—to become self-disciplined and honest—and to therefore become ever more able to perceive the nature of the positive good.

The truth seems painfully simple—so simple that it is a miracle, of sorts, that it can ever be forgotten. Love God, with all thy mind, and all thy acts, and all thy heart. This means, serve truth above all else, and treat your fellow man as if he were yourself—not with the pity that undermines his self-respect, and not with the justice that elevates you above him, but as a divinity, heavily burdened, who could yet see the light.

It is said that it is more difficult to rule oneself than a city, and this is no metaphor. This is the truth, as literal as it can be made. It is precisely for this reason that we keep trying to rule the city.[192]

---

[192] Peterson, *Maps of Meaning*, 454-455.

ABOUT THE AUTHOR

After studying philosophy at Anderson University, Tylor Lovins has been working on a theory of theological language that will express the meanings of religious statements to a secular world. He currently lives in Seattle, WA. You can contact him or follow his work at CultureAndValue.com.

11387964R00089

Printed in Great Britain
by Amazon